Let's look into various issues in Japan and America through films !

映画で見るジェンダー

Masaru Yasuda

Essays by Kimio Ito & Kazuhiro Kunitomo

EIHŌSHA

まえがき

　本書は、日本とアメリカの文化や社会を、ジェンダーを手掛かりに読み解きながら、総合的な英語力を高めることに焦点を絞ったテキストです。ジェンダーと聞くと、難しいし自分とは関係ないと考える人もいるかもしれません。しかし、「男性はこうであるべきだ」とか「女性はこうあるべきだ」といったことを耳にした人もいるのではないでしょうか。このような言い回しの中にも男女にそれぞれの役割を押し付ける構図が垣間見られます。専業主夫・主婦に関わる案件や独身者に対する差別、外見差別やLGBTに関する課題など、ジェンダーの問題は生活の至る所に関わっており、女性だけではなく、男性にも大いに影響するものなのです。世界中で取り組まれているこの問題についての理解を深め、新たな視点を得ることは、日々の生活を送る上でも役立ちますし、全く異なる文化圏で育った人たちと英語でやり取りする際にも有用です。

　学習者の皆さんの取り組みを興味深くするため、本書は伊藤公雄氏（Chapter 1）と、伊藤氏の助言を受けて國友万裕氏（Chapter 2-15）が書き下ろしたエッセイを軸に構成されています。伊藤氏は男性学の権威であり、國友氏は映画とジェンダーが専門で、『マスキュリニティで読む21世紀アメリカ映画』や『インセル時代の男たち　弱者男性で読む日米映画』などの書籍を著しています。これらのエッセイでは、様々なトピックが日本映画とアメリカ映画に言及する形で論じられており、気軽にジェンダーについての考え方を深化させ、日本文化・社会とアメリカ文化・社会の比較考察ができます。また、エッセイ自体は扱われている映画を見ていなくても、その内容を理解できる構成になっていますので、特に映画好きというほどではない人にとっても本書は有用です。もし本書で興味を持った映画があれば実際にその映画を鑑賞することをお勧めします。自主学習の一環として、実際に映画を鑑賞した上で自らの意見を持ち、例えば自らの考えと國友氏の考えを比較検討してみることで、更に理解が深まり、扱われている内容が身近に感じられることでしょう。書かれていることを鵜のみにせず、自らの考えを確立する練習として、本書を活用するのもいいかもしれません。

　本書の各章には、各章のトピックを理解しやすくするための日本語コラムの後、映画の英語タイトルと日本語タイトルを結び付けるPre-Exerciseが置かれています。ここで扱われている映画は、何らかの形でエッセイ内容と関わっています。映画の邦題は、英語を直訳に近い形で翻訳したものや、原題とは関係なく映画の内容を示すものなど様々です。そのようなタイトルが付けられた理由も考えながら取り組んでみましょう。

　続くExercise ①は、エッセイで扱われている映画のうち、2本の要約を取り上げた穴埋め式のリスニングタスクです。要約文を理解することで、後のエッセイ内容が更にわかりやすくなります。文構造なども検討した上で、抜けている箇所に何が入るのかを考えましょう。そうすることで聞き取りの力も更に向上します。

　Exercise ②は、エッセイで使用される語彙に関するタスクです。まずは辞書を使わずに、接頭辞や接尾辞、品詞などを手掛かりにして、英語表現と日本語表現を結び付けてみましょう。知らない表現や忘れていた表現は、ここでしっかりと覚えておくと、エッセイを容易に理解できるようになります。

　エッセイを挟んで、Exercise ③ではエッセイ内容に関するTrue／Falseタスクを行います。エッセイのどのあたりを見れば判断ができるのかを考えながら、TrueかFalseかを検討しましょう。もし選んだ答えが間違っていれば、エッセイに立ち戻って確認するとよいでしょう。そうすることで理解力、読解力が高まります。

Exercise ④は Word Order のタスクです。各章のトピックと関係した文を元に問題が作られており、エッセイの理解を更に深め、英語で議論する際にも役立つ内容が扱われています。文法構造だけでなく、内容についても考えながら、問題に取り組んでみましょう。

　Exercise ⑤は各章で学んだ内容に関する Writing／Discussion タスクです。章の終わりまでに学んだ内容や英語表現などを活用して、自らの考えをアウトプットする課題です。完璧な英語でなくても、問いかけに対して、自分の考えを英語で表現してみましょう。

　本書のエッセイを読み解き、各タスクにしっかりと取り組むことで、ジェンダーという観点から、様々なトピックについての理解を深め、日本とアメリカとの類似点や相違点についての気づきを得ることもできるようになります。本書の内容を契機として、英語力を高め、皆さんが自分なりの考えを構築し、異文化を背景に持つ人たちとこれまで以上に有意義な議論ができる力を身につけ、今後の国際交流に役立ててもらいたいと願っています。

執筆者一同

Contents

テキストの音声は、弊社 HP　https://www.eihosha.co.jp/
の「テキスト音声ダウンロード」のバナーからダウンロードできます。
また、下記 QR コードを読み込み、音声ファイルをダウンロードするか、
ストリーミングページにジャンプして音声を聴くことができます。

本章では、アメリカと日本における「理想の男性像」について考えます。日常生活で「男性は〇〇であるべきだ」と、言われたことや感じたことはありますか。では、一体「理想の男性」とはどのような人のことなのでしょうか。映画や文学作品に登場する主人公を国によって、また年代別で比較することによって、求められている答えが見つかるかもしれません。

PRE-EXERCISE

次の英語の映画タイトルから内容を推測しながら、語群の日本語タイトルと結びつけ、答えを書き入れましょう。

	答え		答え
① *The Big Country* (1958)		④ *The Proud Rebel* (1958)	
② *My Darling Clementine* (1946)		⑤ *Stagecoach* (1939)	
③ *Butch Cassidy and the Sundance Kid* (1969)		⑥ *The Hired Hand* (1971)	

語群

a. 『誇り高き反逆者』　　　　b. 『大いなる西部』

c. 『駅馬車』　　　　　　　　d. 『明日に向って撃て！』

e. 『さすらいのカウボーイ』　f. 『荒野の決闘』

EXERCISE ①

次の文章はリーディング箇所で扱われている映画のあらすじです。文構造や文意を考えながら音声を聴いて、下線部に表現を書き入れてみましょう。

映画❶：『七人の侍』（*Seven Samurai*）

At the end of the Sengoku period, *bushi* turned into (1)_____ repeatedly slaughtered and looted poor farming villages, causing the farmers to (2)_____. The movie follows a group of farmers who cannot (3)_____, but if they continue to be (4)_____ of wheat, they will starve to death. As a solution, the farmers decide to hire samurai to protect their village. With the seven *samurai*, the villagers stand up to protect their village at the risk of their lives.

映画❷：『黄色いリボン』（*She Wore a Yellow Ribbon*）

> Cavalry (1)＿＿＿＿＿＿ Nathan Cutting Brittles, who was about to (2)＿＿＿＿＿＿ in six days due to old age, is given one last mission. His mission is to (3)＿＿＿＿＿＿ the Cheyenne sweep operation while (4)＿＿＿＿＿＿ the captain's wife and niece as they head east. With only four hours left before his retirement, Nathan risked everything he had to defeat the Cheyenne.

EXERCISE ❷ --

次の英語表現と最も意味の近い日本語表現を語群から選び、答えを書き入れてみましょう。

	答え		答え		答え
① particular		⑥ robust		⑪ bond	
② correspond		⑦ significantly		⑫ be perceived as	
③ classify as		⑧ extinguish		⑬ assault	
④ protagonist		⑨ associate		⑭ perspective	
⑤ specialize in		⑩ comradeship		⑮ attempt to	

語群

a. 著しく　　　　　　　b. 特定の　　　　　　　c. 専門に扱う
d. 友情　　　　　　　　e. 結び付ける・連想する　f. 襲撃する・攻撃する
g. 失わせる　　　　　　h. 観点・見方　　　　　　i. （〜を…と）分類する
j. 対応する・該当する　k. たくましい　　　　　　l. 結束・絆
m. 〜しようとする試み　n. 〜として認識される　　o. 主人公

READING --

Every society has its own image of the "ideal man." Comparing the "male image" of Japanese and American films in the 20th century, we can find the "ideal man" for that **particular** era in each society.

When we think of the ideal male image in 20th century movies, we immediately imagine the cowboys in western movies. Many western heroes are memorable, including John Wayne in *She Wore a Yellow Ribbon*, Alan Walbridge in *Shane*, and Clint Eastwood in *A Fistful of Dollars*. Sometimes they are lone wolf types, but most of them are the great fighters and muscular men. Mostly, they are tough, both physically and mentally. This image of the

＊ジョン・ウェイン（1907-1979）：『黄色いリボン』でネイサン・ブリトリス大尉役として主演。
＊アラン・ラッド（1913-1964）：『シェーン』でシェーン役として主演。
＊クリント・イーストウッド（1930-）：『荒野の用心棒』で名無しの男（ジョー）として主演。

cowboy is also beginning to change in the 21st century, and this reminds us of the changing gender situation in the United States.

How about in Japan? In most cowboy movies, the main character is traveling toward the frontier. The **corresponding** image in Japanese film may be the adventures of wandering gamblers (*Matatabi*). That type of genre began with *Kutsukake Tokijirou* and *Mabuta no Haha* by Shin Hasegawa, and continued with the TV drama *Kogarashi Monjiro* in the 1970s. Such traveling gambler stories formed one of the genres of Japanese cinema in the first half of the 20th century. They are stories about a lonely man traveling alone with a secret in his heart. They carry a single *katana* on their waist (which means they're not *samurais*). In modern days, these men would be **classified as** *yakuza*. Basically, the cowboy characters were not beautiful men with some exceptions. On the other hand, many of the Japanese gambler **protagonists** were beautiful.

*股旅物：博徒などが各地を流れ歩く、義理人情の世界を描いたもの。

A beautiful man was probably one of the ideal images of men in Japanese society. This is true not only for the wandering gamblers, but also for the other male heroes like *samurai*. *Samurais* are "organizers" who value clan logic, loyalty, etc., so the genre is a little bit different from the story of lonely gamblers. There is also another variation in the movies of unattached *samurai* that are called *Rounin*.

*浪人者：仕える主君を持たず、他国を流浪している武士。

It may be true that the "beautiful man" tends to be the ideal image of the Japanese man, while American audiences prefer the muscular and tough man. In Japanese *kabuki*, there are two main types of male characters: *Nimaime* (handsome man) and *Tachiyaku* (male roles or the actor who **specializes in** the male roles). According to Tadao Sato, *Nimaime* is more likely to be the main character. Yoshitsune and Benkei are the most typical examples of these two character types. Yoshitsune is slender and beautiful, while Benkei is strong and **robust**. Of course, handsome Yoshitsune is more popular in Japan. Benkei is strong and tough, but he cannot be the main character of the story.

*佐藤 忠男（1940-2022）：日本の映画評論家、編集者。

Even before and after the war, handsome men were rather popular in Japan. However, after the second war, American-style muscular-type men began to appear in Japanese movies. Typical examples would be Toshiro Mifune in *Seven Samurai*, which was remade under the title *The Magnificent Seven* thereby influencing American westerns, or Yujiro Ishihara in *Season of Violence* and *Crazed Fruit*. As a result of the changes in postwar society, the "strong

*三船 敏郎（1920-1997）：『七人の侍』で菊千代役として主演。
*石原 裕次郎（1934-1987）：『狂った果実』で滝島夏久役として主演。

man" who supported high economic growth probably became the ideal image.

However, this trend has also changed **significantly** since around the 1980s. The handsome, slender men often seen in Johnny & Associates, Inc. seem to be more acceptable in modern Japan. The old "beautiful and handsome men" culture is not easily **extinguished**.

By the way, cowboys, gamblers, and even *samurais* are all fighting men. Fighting is important to men in film, in life, and even in the history of mankind. It's about time to end the cultural assumptions that **associates** men with the fight-loving beings.

The relationship between fighting and masculinity also reveals some interesting issues. It is what is called **comradeship** or comrades-in-arms. These words usually indicate a strong **bond** between men in battle. Such strong bonding between men can **be perceived as** "homosexual" as well.

The British literary critic Eve Kosofsky Sedgwick used the term "homosocial" to describe the strong bond between men that differs from homosexuality. She also theorized that homosociality is characterized by homophobia and misogyny. In other words, men exclude women, and then also emphasize that "We are not gay."

While this concept is extremely valid, I think there is another connection between the men that cannot be analyzed by itself, and Sedgwick seemed to have noticed that, too. Although it does not involve sexual intercourse, it is a strong, erotic connection between men who are "willing to die together." The relationship has little to do with homophobia or misogyny. These scenes are quite common in Japanese films, for example, *yakuza* films from the Toei Company. Watching the scene between Ken Takakura and Ryo Ikebe as the two men make an **assault** together with daggers, I don't think it can be analyzed in terms of either homosexuality or homosociality. How about calling this "I would die with you" kind of relationship between men homoeroticism? Some people have made similar arguments about this, though. Another typical example is Akinari Ueda's *The Chrysanthemum Vow* in *Tales of Moonlight and Rain*. *The Chrysanthemum Vow* is a story about a man who dies to keep a promise to meet his friend and comes back to see him across time and space.

Sedgwick has provided an interesting **perspective** on the homosocial in her

*ジャニーズ事務所：日本の芸能プロダクション。

*イヴ・コゾフスキー・セジウィック（1950-2009）：1985年に『男同士の絆―イギリス文学とホモソーシャルな欲望』を出版し、ホモソーシャルという概念を普及させた。
*homophobia：同性愛嫌悪。同性愛に対して差別や偏見など否定的な価値観を持つこと。
*misogyny：女嫌い・女性憎悪。女性や女らしさに対する嫌悪のこと。そのような感情を持つ人のことをmisogynistと言う。
*have little to do with：〜とほとんど関係がない
*dagger：短刀のこと。また、博徒やヤクザが喧嘩の道具として使っていた短刀のことを隠語で「ドス」と言う。
*任侠映画：高倉健と池部良共演による東映の任侠映画の代表作は、『昭和残侠伝』。（全9作）
*上田秋成（1734〜1809）：代表作は『雨月物語』、『諸道聴耳世間狙』など。

study of literary works, and I believe that film can also teach us a new way of looking at society and human relationships. In this sense, I expect that this book's **attempt to** compare Japanese and U.S. masculinity through movies will provide readers with unexpected discoveries.

EXERCISE ③ --

次の各文が、リーディングの内容と一致していれば T を、一致しなければ F を選び、〇をつけましょう。

	答え
① According to the writer, the image of the ideal man varies by country, and stereotypes of male images have been carried over from generation to generation.	T・F
② The writer says that the heroes in western movies are all handsome, tall, and strong in fights.	T・F
③ As the ideal male image for Japanese, it is also important to be beautiful in appearance, and a good-looking man is more likely to be the protagonist of a movie.	T・F
④ The author implies that due to changes in social conditions, tough men like those in American films began to appear in Japanese movies as one of the ideal male images in the postwar period.	T・F
⑤ The writer says that the strong bonds between men seen on the battlefield and other fighting situations can also be regarded as a type of gay relationships.	T・F
⑥ Sedgwick used the term "homosocial" to describe the relationship between men who are willing to risk their own lives to save their fellow.	T・F
⑦ According to the writer, Sedgwick analyzed literary works and cowboy movies to propose the term "homosocial."	T・F

文構造と文の意味を意識しながら、次の［　　］内の表現を並べ替えて、文法的にも意味的にも正しい文を作りましょう。

① Western films are set in the late 19th century American West, mainly [areas / frontiers / in / called / unexplored / the].

② The market for men's cosmetics is expanding in Japan, indicating [men / concerned / more / more / are / and / that / about] their appearance.

③ The period of high economic growth refers to the 19 years from 1955 to 1973, when the Japanese [of / annual rate / at / an / grew / average / economy] 10%.

④ "Achieve gender equality" is one of the Sustainable Development Goals adopted by United Nation to [have / in / ideas / the / that / root / eliminate / taken] society, such as "men should be strong" and "women should be feminine."

⑤ The Stonewall Riots, which occurred on June 28, 1969, [catalyst / regarded / homosexual / are / as / a / the / for] rights movement in the United States and around the world.

⑥ To commemorate [as / declassify / the / homosexuality / WHO's / to / decision] a mental disorder, May 17 was designated as the International Day Against Homophobia, Transphobia and Biphobia.

⑦ Misogyny, literally "hatred of women," [to / aversion / by / men / an / refers / held] or women to women, femininity, and the female gender.

●EXERCISE ⑤：Discussion／Writing --

> 次の問いかけに関して、自分の考えをまとめてみましょう。

① According to the writer, the image of the ideal man has changed throughout the ages. What kind of man do you think is the "ideal man" envisioned by today's Japanese society? Please explain your thoughts along with the reasons why such a man is desired.

② Does the ideal image of women also differ from country to country? Consider the "ideal woman" in Japan and other countries and compare them.

あなたはマッチョな男性に憧れますか?車の運転をする男性は格好良いですか?「控えめに」「優しくサポートし」「メイクして、ハイヒールも履いて」みたいな、これまで求められてきた「女らしさ」を息苦しいと感じる女性は増えています。一方で、「男なら泣くな」「大黒柱なんだから!」「戦え、強くあれ!」みたいな、求められてきた「男らしさ」を、いまの男性はどう受け止めているのでしょうか。「男らしく」あることが「有害」?トキシック・マスキュリニティという言葉について考えてみましょう。

PRE-EXERCISE

次の英語の映画タイトルから内容を推測しながら、語群の日本語タイトルと結びつけ、答えを書き入れましょう。

	答え		答え
① *Magnum Force*（1973）		④ *Throne of Blood*（1957）	
② *The Mule*（2018）		⑤ *Two Mules for Sister Sara*（1970）	
③ *The Seagull*（2018）		⑥ *Invictus*（2009）	

a.『真昼の死闘』 b.『かもめ』

c.『負けざる者たち』 d.『運び屋』

e.『ダーティハリー2』 f.『蜘蛛巣城』

EXERCISE ①

次の文章はリーディング箇所で扱われている映画のあらすじです。文構造や文意を考えながら音声を聴いて、下線部に表現を書き入れてみましょう。

映画❶:『クライ・マッチョ』（*Cry Macho*）

Mike was a rodeo star in Texas, but since his falling from a horse, he （1）＿＿＿＿＿＿ a dull, lonely life. He is asked by a friend to bring back his son Rafael, who is living （2）＿＿＿＿＿＿ in Mexico. Mike, Rafael and a cockfighting rooster named Macho, which Mike teasingly calls a chicken meaning （3）＿＿＿＿＿＿, make their way to the border. Chased by pursuers, they continue their （4）＿＿＿＿＿＿.

映画❷：『ドライブ・マイ・カー』（*Drive My Car*）

> Kafuku, a stage actor, knows that his wife, a scriptwriter, has a secret, but he never (1) _____ it with her and she dies suddenly. Two years later, Kafuku is (2) _____ to direct a play by Chekhov at a (3) _____ and meets his personal driver Misaki. As he faces the play and (4) _____ time in his car, which Misaki drives, he begins to face himself.

❷ EXERCISE ②

次の英語表現と最も意味の近い日本語表現を語群から選び、答えを書き入れてみましょう。

	答え		答え		答え
① star		⑥ term		⑪ metaphor	
② overrate		⑦ curse		⑫ subordinate	
③ exclusively		⑧ interpret		⑬ intervene	
④ equivalent		⑨ initiative		⑭ harassment	
⑤ drastically		⑩ manifestation		⑮ entrust	

語群

a. 解釈する	b. 同等のもの	c. 隠喩・たとえ・象徴
d. 用語	e. 任せる・委託する	f. 表明
g. 劇的に・大幅に	h. 主役を演じる	i. 入り込む・介在する
j. 過大評価する	k. 呪い	l. 嫌がらせをすること・悩ますこと
m. 主導権	n. もっぱら・排他的に	o. 従属する・下位の

❸ READING

Clint Eastwood directed and **starred** in a movie called *Cry Macho* (2021). At the climax of the film, the main character, driving a car, speaks lines that criticize traditional macho men: "This macho thing is **overrated**. You think you got all the answers, then you realize as you get old, that you don't have any of them. By the time you figure it out, it's too late."

Speaking of Eastwood, he gained a reputation in his youth for playing cops in films such as *Dirty Harry* and later moved into directing films, and he was 91 years old when *Cry Macho* was released. In his later years, he has become more prominent as a director than as an actor, but he has **exclusively** made

*クリント・イースト ウッド（1930-）： アメリカ出身の俳 優、監督。

* macho： 通常は 形容詞。名詞は machismo（男らし さ、男性優位主義） が一般的。

*Dirty Harry：刑事ハ リーが活躍するアク ション映画で、シ リーズ化した。

films that evoke an old-fashioned American man. The man is always silent, unsympathetic, and husky-voiced, giving off the melancholy of an old man who can only live an awkward life.

He is typical of a Republican supporter and a macho man in America. It was a surprise to hear him say these lines.

When you go to America, you will see many men wearing cowboy hats. We are made aware that America still retains the traditions of the far West. Western movies were at their height roughly from the 1940s to the 1950s. The heroes of Westerns were the **equivalent** of Japanese samurai warriors, and they were the lone, "Big Bad Wolves."

Metafictional western films are often made these days, such as *No Country for Old Men*, but they have changed **drastically** from the traditional ones. In these films, we have lines that are clearly criticizing the male gender. It is particularly convincing when an elderly man, like Eastwood, says these lines. Probably he has lived his whole life caught up in his masculinity, but in the end, he reflects on how pointless it was.

In the 21st century, we often hear the **term** "toxic masculinity" in America. America is a country with a tradition of Tarzan, so the idea that a man must be masculine and strong both mentally and physically is much more deeply rooted than in Japan. However, around the 1970s, the men's movement arose in America, and the negative aspects of masculinity gradually began to become an issue.

Men are more likely to commit suicide and become shut-in, have more physical illnesses, and have shorter life spans. It is now said that this is due to the fact that they are caught up in toxic masculinity. In the past, there was a belief that if you were a man, you should sweat from your forehead and fight. However, by the end of the 20th century, as environmental problems became more serious, people began to see that men's excessive pursuit of civilization and success had led to environmental destruction. Thus, more and more films are being produced that make us rethink the issue of masculinity.

What about Japan? A movement to consider male gender has existed in Japan since the 1990s. Although Japan is said to be a feminine country, and the **curse** of masculinity is not as strong as in America, men are still more likely to suffer from mental illness than women. Men don't want to face their feelings,

*Republican：共和党支持者。共和党は、民主党と並ぶ現代アメリカの二大政党の一つ。
*cowboy hat：山高でつばが広い帽子。cowboy は牧場労働者のこと。アメリカでよく着用されるのは野球帽や冬のニット帽などだが、これを被る人もある。
*metafictional：metafiction は、物語が「これはフィクション、作り話だ」ということを視聴者や読者に意識させる構造をもつ。

*toxic masculinity：アメリカで使われ始めたとされ、*New York Times* の記事 "What Is Toxic Masculinity?" (2019) が有名。
*Tarzan：アメリカの作家エドガー・ライス・バローズによる小説（1912）の野生児の主役。
*life span：寿命。平均寿命は日本で男性82歳、女性88歳、アメリカで男性77歳、女性82歳（「国連人口基金」2022年版より）。

*mental illness：精神障害、心の病。数としては躁うつ病を含む患者は女性が多いが（厚生労働省2020年度版患者調査より）、一方で自殺率は男性が高い（警視庁 HP より）。

and without realizing it, they don't know what they are feeling.

Drive My Car was the first Japanese film that was nominated for an Academy Award for Best Picture, and Ryusuke Hamaguchi also became the third Japanese director in history to have been nominated for an Academy Award for Directing, a long time since Akira Kurosawa, and won an Academy Award for Best International Feature Film. Many critics have interpreted the film from the viewpoint of "masculinity."

"I should have been hurt properly," says the main character, Kafuku (Hidetoshi Nishijima), near the end of the film. Writer Michiyo Nishimori **interprets** this work as a story in which the main character, a middle-aged man, is freed from "the norms and curses imposed on men, such as not to cry unnecessarily, not to whine, not to rely on others, and to take the **initiative** in everything they do. ("The Story of How He 'Got Hurt Properly' depicted in the film *Drive My Car*")." Here, the film is interpreted as a **manifestation** of the importance of self-care for men.

In the past, it was common for a man to drive and a woman to sit in the passenger seat. This is a **metaphor** for a man living his own life and a woman being **subordinate** to him. Also, a car is a private space where one can be alone, a metaphor for maintaining a certain distance from others in order not to hurt oneself. In fact, the main character tries to ride in the car alone as much as possible. He does not want anyone to ride with him. It could be said that this is a Western-style drama about a man who does not want women to **intervene** in his world.

In the film, his initiative changes through the act of driving. In a scene, to quote Nishimori again, "At the beginning of the film, Kafuku is at the wheel of the car by himself, and he thinks that he is the only one who can be himself in that space. However, after the accident, when his wife, Oto, takes over driving, he does not fully trust her driving, and he tells her what to do, and Oto jokingly says, 'That could be moral **harassment**'."

After the death of his wife, he gets into a car driven by a young female driver named Misaki. At first, he was puzzled because he wanted to drive his car himself, but gradually he comes to **entrust** himself to Misaki's driving. In other words, you can read this as a story about a guy who thought that a man has to control himself and should always take initiative, but who gradually starts

*濱口竜介（1978-）：映画監督、脚本家。国際的な映画祭で様々な賞を受賞。
*黒澤 明（1910-1998）：日本映画を代表する映画監督。国際的にも影響力、評価が高い。

*"The Story of How He 'Got Hurt Properly' depicted in the film *Drive My Car*"：西森路代による映画評「映画『ドライブ・マイ・カー』で描かれる、「正しく傷つく」までの物語」（2021年）。

*at the wheel：ハンドルを握る。wheel は「回転する輪」を意味し、at the wheel で「船の舵輪をとる（舵取りをする）、運転する」となる。タイヤの車輪は複数形 wheels で使われることが多い。

to let a woman take the lead, and eventually comes to realize the problem of toxic masculinity.

It goes without saying that a car is a metaphor for masculinity. The fact that those films were released at the same time in Japan and the U.S. reminds us once again that the time has come to seriously consider the issue of male gender.

*it goes without saying that~：~は言うまでもない。

Now, what will happen to men?

EXERCISE ③ ---

次の各文が、リーディングの内容と一致していれば T を、一致しなければ F を選び、〇をつけましょう。

	答え
① The theme presented by *Cry Macho* and *Drive My Car* is common to that of the western movies at their height in the 1940s and 1950s.	T・F
② Symbols of masculinity in the traditional concepts include being silent, cowboy hats, Tarzan and a male character in the driver's seat.	T・F
③ In *Drive My Car*, Kafuku, who thinks of the driver's seat as his own world under his responsibility, is at first perplexed by the idea of letting a female driver take the wheel.	T・F
④ In the traditional view, a "masculine" person is described as a man who does not cry unnecessarily, does not rely on others, sweats from his forehead and fights, and gets hurt properly.	T・F
⑤ Around the 1970s, the men's movement emerged in the United States, earlier than a similar movement in Japan, and in the 21st century the term "toxic masculinity" appeared in the United States.	T・F
⑥ According to the passage, in the process of becoming unable to drive himself, the main character in *Drive My Car* reconsidered the masculinity he had believed in.	T・F
⑦ The harm that men themselves suffer from toxic masculinity is expressed in their higher frequency of suicide and mental illnesses than women, and in making those around them feel melancholy.	T・F

▶EXERCISE ④：Word Order

文構造と文の意味を意識しながら、次の［　］内の表現を並べ替えて、文法的にも意味的にも正しい文を作りましょう。

① Toxic masculinity has referred to harm inflicted on others, such as arrogant attitudes toward women or minorities who are not considered masculine, but in recent years it [the perspective / been / from / discussed / has also / also harmful / that / it is] to men themselves.

② The film *Drive My Car* [based / of / on / the short / title / story / is / the same] in *Men Without Women*, the short story collection by Haruki Murakami, and also combines elements from other stories in the collection.

③ Haruki Murakami gave a thought-provoking speech in Jerusalem in 2009, saying "Between a high solid wall and a small egg that breaks against it, I will always stand on the side of the egg. Yes, no [may / be, / matter how / the egg, I / the wall / right / will be standing / how wrong] with the egg."

④ The English word "macho" is derived from the Spanish "macho," meaning "male," and [the / of / strong, brave / contains / being / and belligerent etc. / sense], suggesting an excessive masculinity.

⑤ The movie *Gran Torino*, directed by and starring Clint Eastwood, is the name of a car owned by the main character, a retired military veteran, and [a minority group / story / Hmong Americans, / interaction / follows / with / his / the] in the United States.

⑥ "A glass ceiling" refers to barriers within organizations [promote / despite / women and minorities / not / above a certain / do / that / position,] their qualifications and achievements, and is now also used symbolically for practices that prevent minorities, both men and women, from improving their status.

⑦ The Gender Gap Index, an indicator of the imbalance between men and women in the four areas of economy, education, health, and politics, shows Japan in 116th place out of 146 countries as of 2022, the [lower / among / lowest level / countries / and / than / developed] Korea, China, and ASEAN countries in Asia.

ⓔXERCISE ⑤：Discussion／Writing --

> 次の問いかけに関して、自分の考えをまとめてみましょう。

① What "feminine" behaviors and characteristics do you think have traditionally been expected of women, as compared to the traditional "masculinity" expected of men?"

② What changes do you think would occur around you and in our society if people realized that men could be freed from toxic masculinity?

男性が賃金労働を女性が家事労働を担うという性的役割モデルは時代遅れになり、今では多くの女性が仕事を持ち、男性も積極的に家事をすることが求められるようになりました。映画の中でも男性が家事や育児をする場面を見ることが多くなってきましたが、現実にはまだまだ家事や育児の大部分を女性が担っているという指摘もあります。みなさんはどのように感じますか。

Ⓟ PRE-EXERCISE

次の英語の映画タイトルから内容を推測しながら、語群の日本語タイトルと結びつけ、答えを書き入れましょう。

	答え		答え
① *The Theory of Everything*（2014）		④ *What Maisie Knew*（2012）	
② *Moonstruck*（1987）		⑤ *Boyhood*（2014）	
③ *I Don't Know How She Does It*（2011）		⑥ *The Ugly Truth*（2009）	

語群
    a.『6才のボクが、大人になるまで』   b.『博士と彼女のセオリー』
    c.『ケイト・レディが完璧な理由』   d.『男と女の不都合な真実』
    e.『メイジーの瞳』   f.『月の輝く夜に』

Ⓔ EXERCISE ①

次の文章はリーディング箇所で扱われている映画のあらすじです。文構造や文意を考えながら音声を聴いて、下線部に表現を書き入れてみましょう。

映画❶：『老後の資金がありません』（*I Have No Funds for Retirement*）

A housewife who has been saving and (1)＿＿＿＿＿＿ money for retirement is suddenly faced with a turning point. Her father-in-law's (2)＿＿＿＿＿＿, moving in with her mother-in-law, her husband's (3)＿＿＿＿＿＿, and her daughter's wedding preparations all (4)＿＿＿＿＿＿ to drain her precious savings one after another. Will she be happy in her old age?

映画❷：『クレイマー、クレイマー』（*Kramer vs. Kramer*）

> After eight years of marriage, the wife, determined to become
> (1)＿＿＿＿＿, suddenly leaves home, leaving their seven-year-
> old son (2)＿＿＿＿＿. The husband, who had been devoted
> to his job, begins a life of hardship. Just as the bond with his son
> finally (3)＿＿＿＿＿, the wife sues for child support rights, and
> (4)＿＿＿＿＿ begins her and her husband for custody.

❷ EXERCISE ②

次の英語表現と最も意味の近い日本語表現を語群から選び、答えを書き入れてみましょう。

	答え		答え		答え
① expense		⑥ labor force		⑪ breadwinner	
② be laid off		⑦ be subject to		⑫ rationally	
③ infertility		⑧ lag far behind		⑬ outsource	
④ artificial insemination		⑨ figure		⑭ a wide spectrum of	
⑤ make a big splash		⑩ abandon		⑮ gender-equal	

語群

a. 労働力、労働人口　　　　　　　b. 費用、経費
c. 姿、人物、数字、形　　　　　　d. 従う、左右される
e. 稼ぎ手、大黒柱　　　　　　　　f. 合理的に、理性的に
g. 外部調達、委託する　　　　　　h. 解雇される、休職になる
i. 男女平等な、男女同権の　　　　j. 人工受精、人工受胎
k. 大成功する、大きな評判をえる　l. 大きく遅れをとる
m. 広範囲の、幅広い　　　　　　　n. 放棄する、捨てる、立ち退く
o. 不妊、不毛

❷ READING

I was attracted to this film, *I Have No Funds for Retirement*, by the title. The story
is somewhat obvious just by looking at the title. The main character, played
by Amami Yuki, lives with her husband and two children. She is an ordinary
housewife who goes to a yoga class and makes small talk with other women.
However, she ends up taking care of her mother-in-law played by Kusabue
Mitsuko, an old woman who, even in her old age, is very energetic but naive,

falling for the "it's me, it's me" scam and spending money without thinking about the future. On top of that, Amami's daughter is getting married, so she has to shoulder the wedding **expenses**. To make matters worse, her husband **is laid off**. The balance of her bank account is dwindling fast. Realistically speaking, this is a serious situation, but this is a comedy that cheerfully laughs it off.

Most of all, I thought the line "We are both unemployed" was a good one. In the past, it would have been the man who would have to bear the financial responsibility in such a case. Nowadays, that is not necessarily the case. This line shows that working together has become the norm. When the wife receives word that her husband has lost his job, she is more worried about whether he will commit suicide than about the state of the economy. This is also good. Just because a man loses his job does not mean he has to kill himself. In the past, if a man lost his job, it would have been a matter of life or death, but now we must free him from that kind of bondage.

When Amami's husband goes to Hello Work to look for a job, the phrase "a man who only knows the same company" comes up, making it difficult for him to get a new job. During the high economic growth period, staying with one company would have been the way to get ahead, but we come to realize that this is no longer the case. As expected, the film ends with the conclusion that happiness is possible even without money. The 21st century is an era in which the idea of men working in a career and women staying at home has started to disappear.

Hikita-san, You Are Pregnant is a film that is like a manual for raising a child. Since men cannot have children, they have no knowledge of **infertility** or **artificial insemination**. It is a film that makes us understand that having and raising a child is a shared work.

What Did You Eat Yesterday? is new in that it depicts the lives of gay men through cooking. The film makes us think that the current trend of men becoming more homemaker-like, perhaps because it is difficult to find fulfillment in their work, may be true.

In *Step*, Takayuki Yamada plays a single father. In *And Then the Baton Was Passed*, Kei Tanaka also plays a single father, and the scene where he casually cooks the dishes shows how the times have changed. Nowadays, it is not

*"it's me, it's me" scam：オレオレ詐欺、電話で身内などと思い込ませ、窮状を訴え現金を振り込ませる詐欺。

*Hello Work：公共職業安定所、就職や転職を希望する人に仕事を紹介してくれる行政機関。
*high economic growth period：高度成長期、1955年から1973年まで、日本が年間平均10%の経済成長をした時期。

*homemaker：ジェンダー・ニュートラルな言葉としてhousewifeやhousehusbandに代わって広く使われる。

unusual for men to do housework; it is an everyday scene.

I wonder how this is in the U.S. Speaking of men and housework in the U.S., there is a great movie called *Kramer vs. Kramer* which caused a social phenomenon. After that, however, there was *I Am Sam* and a few others, but I don't think there have been any films that have **made a big splash**.

According to Kimio Ito, male cabin attendants and women porters were introduced to the U.S. in the 1970's. In 1970, Japan's female **labor force** participation rate was much higher than that of the U.S.; second only to Finland and a little higher than Sweden which was third place. Thus, Japan's equality index was high enough to be on par with Scandinavia.

Furthermore, according to Ito, unlike in the West, where women were the object of protection, Japan was a society where women were expected to work as a matter of course: they **were subject to** both independence and subordination. (Changes in Scandinavia started in the late 1960s, so if we take 1960 as the year of comparison, Japanese women's labor participation would probably have been the highest in societies with fairly-well-developed economies. This has not changed since the first half of the 20th century. Unlike the United States and the United Kingdom, where more than 80% of women did not work, Japan was by far the leader with more than 60% in the first half of the 20th century.)

Japan is now considered to have a larger gender gap than the West because Japan **lagged far behind** during the sexual revolution of the 1970s.

When it comes to family stories, the U.S. seems to lean more toward those depicting father-son relationships. One reason for this may be that the U.S. is a Christian country that prefers stories about father **figures** and young men, such as the 21st century film *We Bought a Zoo*, in which a man played by Matt Damon who lost his wife revives an abandoned zoo with his two children. This film is indeed about a man raising his children, but there are almost no scenes of cooking or cleaning. Rather, the focus is on the son's attempts to recover from the loss of his mother. It is a typical father-son film.

In the United States, there are men who do housework, such as Frances McDormand's husband in *Fargo*, Julia Roberts' boyfriend in *Erin Brockovich*, and Anne Hathaway's husband in *The Intern*, but they are only supporting characters, and I can't think of many in which the househusband is the center

*伊藤公雄（1951年-）：日本の社会学者で大阪大学、京都大学名誉教授。専門分野は、男性学、ジェンダー論、メディア研究など。

*equality index：平等指数、ここでは労働人口数における男女の平等について述べている。ただし労働形態や賃金、あるいは他の分野の男女平等については言及していない。

*sexual revolution：1960年代にアメリカやヨーロッパで始まった従来の性や性行動に対する社会通念からの解放運動。

*lean toward：～の方に傾く、傾向がある

of the story.

Marriage Story is a modern version of *Kramer vs. Kramer* and depicts divorce proceedings. Although there is still the custom of men being the **breadwinner** and women supporting them, women are not necessarily seen as more suitable for childcare, and it has become the norm for women to work and men to do the housework and childcare.

Americans do not spend as much time and money on housework as in Japan. Westerners are surprised at the Japanese bento boxes. While in Japan, children are given character bento with carefully crafted emoji, in the U.S., children are simply given peanut butter sandwich in plastic wrap. In the morning, each child eats a bowl of cereal with milk poured over it. The wife of an American teacher I know is Japanese, and she told me that the good thing about being married to him is that she doesn't have to worry about serving the same thing every day. While Japanese people try to change the menu every day, Americans are fine with a hamburger every day.

*character bento：キャラ弁、アニメのキャラクターなどをモチーフにして作るお弁当。

The American mindset is that cooking and cleaning should be done **rationally** and childcare may be **outsourced** to people outside the family to encourage children's ability to cope with **a wide spectrum of** people, which is probably the main difference between Japan and the U.S. Japanese people are more disciplined and believe that they must put their heart and soul into their work, so they continue to make character bento. This mindset to please others with quality may be one of the strengths of the Japanese people, but it seems to be one of the obstacles in promoting a **gender-equal** society. Now, will Japanese people be able to outsource housework and child-rearing in the future?

*disciplined：ここでは「律儀な」という趣旨で使われている。

*child-rearing：子育て

ⓔXERCISE ③ --

次の各文が、リーディングの内容と一致していればＴを、一致しなければＦを選び、〇をつけましょう

	答え
① The writer argues that not only husbands but also wives feel responsible for their family financial situations these days.	T・F
② According to the writer, continuing to work for the same company for decades is seen as a strength.	T・F

	答え
③ The writer thinks the number of movies depicting men and housework is fewer in the U.S. than in Japan.	T・F
④ If parents outsource childcare, their children will have less opportunities to meet various types of people.	T・F
⑤ Hello Work is a place where you can get support when you seek for an employment.	T・F
⑥ Artificial insemination is a medical treatment offered to couples who do not want to have children.	T・F
⑦ The writer points out that Japanese people's mindset to please others with quality could have a negative effect on gender equality.	T・F

●EXERCISE ④：Word Order

文構造と文の意味を意識しながら、次の〔　〕内の表現を並べ替えて、文法的にも意味的にも正しい文を作りましょう。

① Housework should include〔 not / also / cleaning and cooking / but / only 〕childcare, tutoring, yard work, repairing broken house parts, car maintenance and so forth.

② Sometimes films about homosexual couples〔 gay men / up / of / stereotypes / reinforcing / end 〕.

③ For〔 men / solely through / had / their lives / lived / work / who 〕, the loss of their jobs meant a major identity crisis.

④ In response to the excessive character lunchbox competition, some kindergartens〔 are / making one / from / to refrain / parents / asking 〕.

⑤ [gender equality / reports / in / Gender Gap Index / The World Economic Forum's] politics, economics, education, and health.

⑥ Gender, which is socially defined masculinity and femininity, [has / over time / and / changed / subject to change / is] in the future.

⑦ We need to promote [while also / acknowledging / to prevent / birthrates / measures / declining] family diversity.

EXERCISE ⑤ : Discussion／Writing

次の問いかけに関して、自分の考えをまとめてみましょう。

① Japan has been ranked below 100 out of 144 countries in the Gender Gap Index published by the Economic Forum for the past several years, what do you think is the main cause?

② What do you think companies need to do to increase the rate of male employees taking parental leave? How responsible should employers be for the well-being of employees and their families?

「イクメン」とは育児をするメンズ、つまり育児に積極的に関わる男性のことを指します。「イクメン」という言葉は、2010年には流行語大賞にもランクインするなど、今や日本社会に広く浸透しています。みなさんは、身近なところで「イクメン」を多く見かけますか？では「イクメン」は、英語ではどのように表現するのでしょうか？英語圏の国々では、父親が育児に積極的に参加するのはごく自然なことなので、「イクメン」という表現自体が存在しません。基本的に「イクメン」であることが普通の父親の姿なのでしょう。「イクメン」や「イクメンプロジェクト」という表現が特別に存在する日本を、社会全体で変えていかないといけないのかもしれません。

PRE-EXERCISE

次の英語の映画タイトルから内容を推測しながら、語群の日本語タイトルと結びつけ、答えを書き入れましょう。

	答え		答え
① *Father of the Bride*（1991）		④ *Any Day Now*（2012）	
② *Sleepless in Seattle*（1993）		⑤ *The Pursuit of Happyness*（2006）	
③ *Fathers and Daughters*（1995）		⑥ *Nowhere Special*（2020）	

 語群

a. 『いつか君にもわかること』　　b. 『パパが遺した物語』

c. 『幸せのちから』　　d. 『めぐり逢えたら』

e. 『花嫁のパパ』　　f. 『チョコレートドーナツ』

EXERCISE ①

次の文章はリーディング箇所で扱われている映画のあらすじです。文構造や文意を考えながら音声を聴いて、下線部に表現を書き入れてみましょう。

映画❶：『総理の夫』（*First Gentleman*）

One day, Rinko, the wife of ornithologist Hiyori Soma, asks Hiyori, "If I became prime minister..." Hiyori did not (1)＿＿＿＿＿＿ this and went on a birding trip, spending 10 days on an isolated island. However, the world changed (2)＿＿＿＿＿＿ during that time. Rinko was (3)＿＿＿＿＿＿ the first female prime minister in history. Simultaneously, Hiyori becomes the "First Gentleman," Hiyori decides to support his beloved wife, but finds himself caught up in unexpected (4)＿＿＿＿＿＿.

映画❷：『ひとりじゃない、わたしたち』（*Together Together*）

> Matt, a single, male app developer in his 40s, asks 26-year-old Anna to be a（1）＿＿＿＿＿＿＿＿ for his child. Ana agrees, thinking she can get a college degree（2）＿＿＿＿＿＿. As the birth approaches, Matt's passion for parenthood grows and he begins to （3）＿＿＿＿＿＿ in Ana's life. Ana is annoyed with Matt, but gradually comes to find him（4）＿＿＿＿＿＿＿＿. The two self-proclaimed loners gradually begin to open up to each other and develop an unexpected friendship.

EXERCISE ②

次の英語表現と最も意味の近い日本語表現を語群から選び、答えを書き入れてみましょう。

	答え		答え		答え
① favorable		⑥ conventional		⑪ custody	
② in vogue		⑦ satirize		⑫ abuse	
③ inversion		⑧ fuss		⑬ well suited for	
④ physical well-being		⑨ underscore		⑭ significant	
⑤ drastically		⑩ preconceptions		⑮ streamlined	

語群

a. 慣例的な	b. 大騒ぎ	c. 親権
d. ～によく適している	e. 流行して	f. 健康
g. 虐待	h. 風刺する	i. 強調する
j. 重要な	k. 先入観	l. 逆転
m. 合理化された	n. 好ましい	o. 大幅に

READING

I was searching the internet sites and it seems that Kei Tanaka has been chosen as the actor with the most beautiful muscles. He's always played the part of a guy with a cute vibe, and I don't see him as masculine in character. Maybe this imbalance between body and character is a **favorable** feature. His face is cute, but his body is muscular. That type of person has been called a momchan in Korea for a long time now. Japan is in the midst of a Korean entertainment boom these days, and actors with Korean faces（e.g., Kentaro

Sakaguchi) seem to be **in vogue**. The center of Asian popular culture is now South Korea rather than Japan.

I recently watched *First Gentleman*, starring Kei Tanaka. The title and poster alone give a general idea of the content, which is clearly a gender **inversion**. It is about Japan's first female prime minister, played by Miki Nakatani. And Kei Tanaka plays her husband.

That is to say, Kei Tanaka plays a man who is married to a woman (the prime minister) who is socially superior to him, yet is also a family man who cares about his wife's **physical well-being**. It is a comedy of gender inversion that focuses on the part of a man who supports a woman's work. In the TV drama *Ossan's Love*, Kei Tanaka played a man in a homosexual relationship without any unnaturalness. Moreover, in that drama, he played the role of a man who was a cabin attendant (CA), a **conventional** female occupation. He is someone who is very **well suited for** such a role.

*That is to say：即ち

This is of course an attempt to **satirize** a society in which the barriers between gender and sexuality are disappearing, but the beauty of the film and TV drama is that they do not emphasize this part of the story. The fact that he is in a romantic relationship with the same sex, that he is a male cabin attendant and that his wife has a higher social status than him, are not portrayed as special and serious, but rather in a natural and lighthearted manner.

In *First Gentleman*, pregnancy, childbirth, and childcare issues arise for the prime minister and first gentleman later in the film. The situation is leaked and becomes public. This **underscores** the fact that women, even as prime ministers, are the child-bearing sex. In another scene, the prime minister says, "I am uncomfortable with all the **fuss** over being a woman." This is a standard line. *In short, the gender inversion involves some women-specific issues, but I find it pleasant that there is no special emphasis on the fact that they are out of the norm.

*In short: 要するに
*gender inversion：
男女の反転

Kei Tanaka also plays a role similar to this in *And Then the Baton Was Passed* (2021), directed by Satoshi Maeda. He is the father of the heroine, played by Meiku Nagano, but he is actually the step father of the heroine, and he lives alone with his daughter, who is not related to him by blood. He, the father, is responsible for housework. I have heard that when men divorce and seek **custody** of their daughters, even if they are the biological fathers, they may be

*biological father：
生物学上の父、実の
父

at a disadvantage compared to women because of concerns about possible sexual **abuse**. In the case of Kei Tanaka in this film, however, he is not even the heroine's biological father, but her stepfather. This would have made the possibility of sexual abuse even higher than that of the biological father. Even so, it was such a heartwarming sight, The scenes of two people living together who are not related by blood make us aware of a new era.

Many men are not sexually abusive, even if they live with children unrelated by blood at home under one roof. In *My Daddy* (2021, directed by Junichi Kanai), a daughter who was raised thinking she was her father's biological daughter turns out not to be his biological child after a test. However, this does not change his parental love for her, nor change his respect for her sexual independence.

Sexual issues are very **significant** for men to deal with as well. It is generally believed that men have stronger sexual urges than women, and this makes men look bad. Because the majority think that if the person with custody were a man, whether the daughter is an adopted child or a biological child, would be inclined to abuse his child sexually. However, the men portrayed in recent films have been portrayed in manners that are by no means sexually exploitive. Today's men are so gentle with women because they have been raised from childhood to be taught that men and women are equal and that they should not sexually abuse women. Therefore, it is time to set aside biased **preconceptions** about being a man, and to solve problems on an individual level, but it is probably difficult to individualize the situation to that extent in reality.

I saw an American movie called *Together Together* (2021, directed by Nicole Beckwith), which is about a single man in his 40s who tries to have a surrogate mother bear his child. This man, by the way, who is not gay, just wants to have a child. In old times, there would have been stories of women not getting married and only wanting children, but I wonder if such a person would have been portrayed as a man. The sex of the child is not yet known until it is born. I wonder how this is perceived in the U.S. In the U.S., the number of films that focus on the theme of gender role reversal seems to have decreased recently compared to Japan. This is because, as mentioned in the previous chapter, the American perspective on the family has changed **drastically** from that of Japan.

＊stepfather：義理の父

＊urge：衝動

＊previous：前の、以前の

According to a website article written by a Japanese working mother in the US
(https://nano-trends.net/working-mom-in-us/),
the U.S. greatly contrasts with Japan in the following particular areas.

No concern for taking time off work for child reasons.
Both husbands and wives work very little overtime.
There is a lot of available daycare space, so children can be placed easily.
No need to take crowded trains（easy commute）.
Almost no evening socializing for work.
No insensitive meddling by anyone.
Older women are comfortable working without worrying about age.
Not associating "domestic work" with love.

Compared to Japan, childcare and work are more **streamlined** in the United States. Although more and more companies in Japan now require their employees to properly use their paid time off, the Japanese value of putting in more time and effort than necessary at home and at work, and the need to be selfless and dedicated, has probably not completely disappeared. Now, how will Japan change over the years?

EXERCISE ③ --

次の各文が、リーディングの内容と一致していれば T を、一致しなければ F を選び、○をつけましょう。

	答え
① According to the writer, Japan is experiencing a Korean craze these days, but the center of Asian popular culture in the 19th century was Japan rather than Korea.	T・F
② Ken Tanaka plays a homely man devoted to his wife in *First Gentleman*.	T・F
③ In the movie *And Then the Baton Was Passed*, the father, played by Kei Tanaka, lives alone with his biological daughter after his divorce.	T・F
④ Stories of men not getting married and only wanting kids have been common in the movies for a long time now.	T・F
⑤ Ken Tanaka often appeared in gender-reversal comedies, and in one drama he played the role of a man in a homosexual relationship.	T・F
⑥ The writer says that Japanese men are taught from childhood that it is impractical to achieve equality between men and women.	T・F
⑦ In Japan, there is a strong sense of value that one must put in more time and effort than necessary, both at home and at work, and work hard.	T・F

EXERCISE ④ : Word Order

文構造と文の意味を意識しながら、次の [　] 内の表現を並べ替えて、文法的にも意味的にも正しい文を作りましょう。

① The term "ikumen" [by / "childcare" / was / and / the words / coined / combining] "good-looking men."

② The Ministry of Health, Labor and Welfare launched the "Ikumen Project" in 2010 to [in / and / encourage housework / to / participate / fathers] childcare.

③ In the past, the [of / the Japanese /main / considered / was / father/ role] to be that of breadwinner for the family.

④ In Japan, absolute dedication to one's [the ideal / work / for / used / considered / be / to] men.

⑤ In English-speaking countries, the expression "ikumen" [quite / it / not / because / exist / does / natural / is] for fathers to actively participate in child-rearing.

⑥ In Japan, even if men want to be more involved in housework and childcare, it is often more difficult for them [work style / of / to / flexible / be / in / terms] and hours compared to women.

⑦ Some women find it [heroic / men / treatment / frustrating / receive / that] simply for doing a minimal share of the routine household chores.

EXERCISE ⑤：Discussion／Writing --

次の問いかけに関して、自分の考えをまとめてみましょう。

① What do you think would help increase the birthrate in Japan?

② Do you consider that many men around you, including your family, neighbors, etc., are ikumen? Why/ Why not?

Chapter 05 Sports

皆さんは、中高時代に、様々な先生との出会いがあったことでしょう。時には、厳し過ぎる先生から、熱心な指導を受けたことがあったかもしれません。大学生になり、過去を振り返ってみると、どんなことが印象に残っていますか。ここでは、主にスポーツの監督や体育の先生がテーマとなった映画に触れ、リーディングを読み、関連した語彙や表現を学び、知識を深め、自分の意見を構築しましょう。そして、紹介された映画（動画）を視聴し、理想的な教師像（監督像）について、考えてみましょう。

PRE-EXERCISE

次の英語の映画タイトルから内容を推測しながら、語群の日本語タイトルと結びつけ、答えを書き入れましょう。

	答え		答え
① *The Heart of the Game*（2005）		④ *Dead Poets Society*（1989）	
② *Remember The Titans*（2000）		⑤ *Friday Night Lights*（2004）	
③ *Mr. Holland's Opus*（1995）		⑥ *The Karate Kid*（1984）	

語群

a. 『いまを生きる』 b. 『陽のあたる教室』
c. 『プライド　栄光への絆』 d. 『タイタンズを忘れない』
e. 『ベスト・キッド』 f. 『女バス』

EXERCISE ①

次の文章はリーディング箇所で扱われている映画のあらすじです。文構造や文意を考えながら音声を聴いて、下線部に表現を書き入れてみましょう。

映画❶：『泣くな赤鬼』（*Don't Cry, Mr. Ogre*）

The story focuses on the reunion and their emotional （1）_____ between a zealous baseball club coach and a former student. He used to be a harsh and coercive teacher known as the red devil, who gave （2）_____ instructions. However, when he learns that his reunited student has only six months to live, the film depicts the teacher's emotional （3）_____ as he reflects on those days and （4）_____ his student again.

映画❷：『恐怖のセンセイ』（*The Art of Self-Defense*）

> The story begins when a（1）_____ man is attacked by a gang and starts attending a karate dojo. He becomes so（2）_____ in karate that he is even fired from his job. Eventually, he is brainwashed by his instructor's overzealousness and takes（3）_____ on the robber. Consequently, it ends up being a mistake. In a sense, this is a black comedy about "macho（4）_____."

ⒺXERCISE ②

次の英語表現と最も意味の近い日本語表現を語群から選び、答えを書き入れてみましょう。

	答え		答え		答え
① legendary		⑥ enthusiasm		⑪ intimidate	
② veritable		⑦ yell at		⑫ vicissitude	
③ paradigm		⑧ confrontation		⑬ embodiment	
④ oppressive		⑨ controversy		⑭ sway	
⑤ manipulate		⑩ ultimately		⑮ condemn	

語群

a. 熱意	b. 操作する	c. 真の
d. 論争	e. 浮き沈み	f. 枠組み、パラダイム
g. 化身	h. 揺り動かす	i. 伝説的な
j. 〜を怖がらせる	k. 〜を怒鳴る	l. 糾弾する
m. 高圧的な	n. 最終的に	o. 対立

ⓇEADING

Recently, a group of people on SNS, so-called Netizens, have been discussing whether or not Ittetsu Hoshi in "The Star of the Giants," the father of the protagonist Hyuma, is an abusive parent. *The Star of the Giants* is a Japanese **legendary** sports manga with a **veritable** cult following. The **paradigm** of the world has changed enormously over the past 50 years.

In 2019, a Japanese movie titled *Don't Cry, Red Devil* was released in theaters. This movie is a drama about a high school baseball team coach and his students. The teacher, played by Shinichi Tsutsumi, coaches the baseball team. As can be inferred from his nickname the "red devil," he is set up as an

*『巨人の星』：原作：梶原一騎・作画：川崎のぼるによる、野球少年の成長を題材にした漫画（1961-1971）。

*SNS：Social Networking Service の略称で、インターネット上で個人同士が繋がることができる場所を提供しているサービスの総称。

oppressive teacher resembling an ogre, or in other words, as a traditional physical education teacher (just like Hyuma's father).

*physical education：体育

But that was in the past. Now he is teaching at a high school with no **enthusiasm** for baseball and is somewhat discouraged. This film is about his accidental reunion with his former student (Yuya Yagira) at the hospital, where they face each other again and reflect on their previous relationship.

As can be easily predicted, there are some reminiscing scenes in which the red devil teacher **yells at** his students. These scenes suggest that the drama might be going to glorify this kind of teacher and make audiences feel uneasy about the rest of the story. However, as the film goes on, it gradually becomes clear that this will not be the case.

*reminiscing scenes：回想場面

The student he reunites with is incurably ill and has little time left to live, but he is the only student who rebelled against Mr. Akaoni, the red devil, during his high school period, quitting the baseball team and dropping out of school. His relationship with Mr. Akaoni is the focal point of the story. In other words, it is not a story of affirming the egomaniacal dogmatic teacher, but rather a story of this teacher becoming self-reflective through his relationship with a male student with whom he had a **confrontation**.

*rebel against：〜に反抗する

What is more, another student, once an honorable student on the baseball team and now a serious businessman, comes up with the line, "We were just tools to make the teacher's dream come true." He was the type of student who obediently followed his teacher, but after standing and thinking for a while, he realized that there was, after all, a problem with Mr. Akaoni's teaching philosophy.

*line：セリフの一節

The physical education teacher problem has long been a major Japanese school **controversy**. Masaru Okazaki, who was himself a physical education teacher, criticizes former physical education teachers in his book, *Let's Blow Up the Physical Education Teachers*. There were a large number of former PE teachers who, today, would have to be dismissed on disciplinary charges. What they were doing was truly power harassment, moral harassment, and sexual harassment of male students. As a result, those students must have had their souls broken. However, until about 40 years ago, when the teacher was considered absolute, the students had no choice—they had to cry by themselves.

*岡崎 勝 著（1986）『体育教師をぶっ飛ばせ』：著者の岡崎勝は、体育教師としての教歴を持つ。

As described in Sandra Haefelin's book, *Physical Education: The Disease That Undermines Japan*, the problem with Japanese society is "gut feeling and peer pressure." If the students are **intimidated** by a physical education teacher, who is a bundle of masculinity, they will be forced to obey him or her. There are certainly some boys, like the former respectful students in this film, who realized "that something was wrong and that they were being used as toys by the teacher," but they had no choice but to follow him because of his intimidating power and peer pressure.

I wonder if those teachers back then have reflected on what they did, just like Mr. Akaoni in this film. Those teachers who were outrageously dictatorial at the time must have had their ups and downs, and gone through many **vicissitudes** as teachers. Unlike 40 years ago, there are many children who are not attending school now. Athletic clubs, too, will surely face trouble—if they stick to the old traditional way of doing things. I wonder if the teachers of the past have also matured along with the changes in society.

What is interesting about this film is the ambivalent feelings shared by the red devil and his dying student. Both of them feel repulsed by each other, but at the same time, they are attracted to each other in a somewhat homosexual way. For them both, the other is probably the **embodiment** of what they have repressed. In general, men who harass others are timid. They feel insecure unless they constantly exaggerate their power over those who are in a weaker position than they are. If even one person disobeys the harasser, his identity will be **swayed**, and he will thunder down on the disobedient person and create an atmosphere in which those around him will not be able to resist. The dying pupil in this film is aware of this weakness in the red devil. That is why the red devil is so worried about him. It is a complicated feeling toward a being who seems to perceive his own mind, which sublimates into something homosexual.

After the former defiant student dies young, he becomes an unforgettable legendary figure for the red devil. Mr. Akaoni has no choice but to go on with his life, bearing his personal experience with the student somewhere deep in his heart.

There is also an American film called *The Art of Self-Defense*. This film also depicts the domination and violence of a seemingly macho and masculine karate sensei. He tries to **manipulate** people around him and pushes them

*サンドラ・ヘフェリン（1975-）：日本を拠点とするドイツ出身の作家、著述家、タレント。
*gut feeling and peer pressure：根性論と同調圧力

*go through：経験する

*mature：成長する

*sublimate：昇華する

*push through：押し通す

through even the most unreasonable things.

What these teachers lack is sentiment above all. Predatory men put their own convenience over that of the others. Surviving by the logic of the weak and the strong, they have become indifferent to breaking the hearts and hurting the self-esteem of those who are weaker than they are. In this film, as the teacher's instruction escalates, the protagonist complains that he can no longer control even his own emotional states. A person with decent sensibilities would not be able to emotionally follow the guidance of such a teacher.

*decent sensibility：
まともな感受性

The United States is an individualistic society. There is less peer pressure than in Japan, and the guts mentality or the die-hard spirit is also supposed to be weaker than in Japan. Yet, the "macho" tradition, the tradition of worshipping physical, muscular beauty, is much more prevalent there. At first sight, the macho teacher appears to be sort of attractive. However, *The Art of Self-Defense* **ultimately** ends up killing this teacher. It is a cruel consequence.

*cruel：残酷な

It is said that Japan is a culture of shame and America is a culture of sin, but in the Japanese film, the student dies and inflicts a shame on his teacher that will never fade away, while in the American film, the teacher is **condemned**. The outcomes are completely opposite, but either way, the message is still the same: coercive and abusive education should be denounced.

*fade away：消える

Certainly, masculinity is beginning to be criticized. It is time for teachers and students to respect each other as more equal individuals.

●EXERCISE ③ --
次の各文が、リーディングの内容と一致していればTを、一致しなければFを選び、〇をつけましょう

	答え
① People actively involved in the net community have assumed that Ittetsu Hoshi, in "The Star of the Giants," is a decades-long ideal parent.	T・F
② In Japanese movies and stories, traditional physical education teachers are described as tyrannical and dogmatic.	T・F
③ The writer claims that because of physical education teachers' threats, the only thing the students could do was to give in to orders.	T・F

	答え
④ The "macho" or "masculinity" tradition has been rejected by almost all cultures worldwide.	T・F
⑤ On the whole, men who are abusive towards their peers seem to be uneasy and lack self-confidence.	T・F
⑥ In the United States, maintaining group-consciousness and integrity is valued in society.	T・F
⑦ The passage implies that there still remain a number of problems between teachers and students in Japanese education.	T・F

EXERCISE ④ : Word Order

文構造と文の意味を意識しながら、次の ［　　］ 内の表現を並べ替えて、文法的にも意味的にも正しい文を作りましょう。

① Physical education, music, and art are considered to be secondary subjects, ［ can / lead / growth / which / to / children's ］.

② Traditionally, ［ used / in Japanese / teachers' guidance / compulsory education, students / to / obey ］ in both the classroom and the club activities after school.

③ Even in the 21st century, ［ regarded / has / as / been / strongly male-dominated / a / society / Japan ］, which causes gender discrimination in public and in private.

④ On the other hand, as women gain a stronger voice, masculinity has been weakening, yet ［ their opinions / men / assert / try / some / to ］.

⑤ Recently, ［ of / has / soldiers / been / the number / markedly increasing / female ］, which seems to negatively affect masculinity in some ways.

⑥ There may be a major difference between masculinity in Japan and in the United States: whereas Japanese masculinity is relevant to mentality, [physical / counterpart / is / more related / strength / the American / to].

⑦ Although [gender / for / have / explored / the past several decades / studies / undoubtedly been], there has been little research specifically in the field of masculinity in Asian countries.

EXERCISE ⑤ : Discussion／Writing --

次の問いかけに関して、自分の考えをまとめてみましょう。

① In Japanese society, sports players such as Olympic athletes are forced to train extremely hard, even though they may have mental health issues. In addition, they sometimes have to sacrifice their privacy to achieve victory. What do you think about this situation?

② What kind of relationship between a teacher and students is the most proper? Please explain your thoughts along with your reasons.

Chapter 06 Fighting Men

男らしさを象徴する要素とはどのようなものでしょうか。それは映画や小説の中でどのように描写されるでしょう。国や時代に関係なく普遍的に認められるものはあるのでしょうか。本章ではこのような問いかけに関するトピックが扱われます。まずは自分が思い描く「男らしい姿」とはどんなものか考えてみるとよいでしょう。そのような人物が登場する映画やドラマはありますか。しかしつくられた作品が描写する「らしさ」はしばしば誇張され、実態とはかけ離れた姿として描かれることがあります。そこから私たちは何を読み解くことができるのかじっくり考えてみましょう。

PRE-EXERCISE

次の英語の映画タイトルから内容を推測しながら、語群の日本語タイトルと結びつけ、答えを書き入れましょう。

	答え		答え
① *Somebody Up There Likes Me*（1956）		④ *All or Nothing*（2002）	
② *The Guardian*（2006）		⑤ *The Blind Side*（2009）	
③ *Billy Elliot*（2000）		⑥ *Bleed for This*（2016）	

語群

a.『幸せの隠れ場所』　　　　b.『リトル・ダンサー』

c.『ビニー／信じる男』　　　d.『傷だらけの栄光』

e.『人生は、時々晴れ』　　　f.『守護神』

EXERCISE ①

次の文章はリーディング箇所で扱われている映画のあらすじです。文構造や文意を考えながら音声を聴いて、下線部に表現を書き入れてみましょう。

映画❶：『ブルー』（*BLUE*）

Nobuto Urita, a professional boxer who deeply loves boxing but keeps losing his fights, is（1）＿＿＿＿＿＿ a successful boxer, Kazuki Ogawa. In an important match, Ogawa defeats Urita, but is struck by the punch-drunker（2）＿＿＿＿＿＿. Ogawa wins both the championship belt and his marriage to Chika Amano, but fails to defend his belt in（3）＿＿＿＿＿＿ matches. However, their fighting spirit as boxers continues to（4）＿＿＿＿＿＿ in their hearts.

映画❷：『ロッキー』(*Rocky*)

Despite his true (1)＿＿＿＿＿＿, Rocky Balboa is a struggling boxer. In the meantime, Apollo Creed, the heavyweight world champion, chooses Rocky as his (2)＿＿＿＿＿＿. With their (3)＿＿＿＿＿＿ support from Paulie, Mickey and his beloved Adrian, Rocky accomplishes the grueling training. As the fight concludes, Creed's superior skill is countered by Rocky's (4)＿＿＿＿＿＿ spirit and his inability to admit defeat.

EXERCISE ②

次の英語表現と最も意味の近い日本語表現を語群から選び、答えを書き入れてみましょう。

	答え		答え		答え
① considerably		⑥ unique		⑪ sneak	
② formation		⑦ acclaim		⑫ drip	
③ depiction		⑧ somber		⑬ pioneering	
④ rule the roost		⑨ solitude		⑭ in succession	
⑤ intellect		⑩ path		⑮ poverty	

語群

a. 唯一の・類のない　　b. 牛耳る　　　　　　c. 孤独
d. 相次いで・連続して　e. こっそり取る　　　f. どんよりした・重苦しい
g. 喝采する・賞賛する　h. 草分け的な・先駆の　i. 貧しさ・貧困
j. 形成　　　　　　　　k. したたる・垂れ流す　l. 描写
m. 道のり・経路　　　　n. かなり・大幅に　　　o. 知性

READING

According to Kimio Ito, Japan during the 300 years of the Heian period and 250 years of the Tokugawa period was an unusual society. Although war was not entirely absent, the "manliness" of the Heian aristocrats probably did not include "fighting." In fact, "fighting" was the culture of "lower" men. Also, in East Asia, not only in Japan, the status of the warrior class is **considerably** lower than that of the literate class. He said that "civilian weakness" may have been the culture of the "truly manly man." In other words, in Japan, macho was lower in the male hierarchy.

*warrior class：武人・武士階級

*civilian weakness：文弱。文事ばかりにふけって弱々しいさま。

Europe, on the other hand, is a society that was at war almost continuously from the fall of the Roman Empire to the mid-20th century, including with respect to religion. In this sense, macho is a Western form of masculinity. Western-style masculinity is not necessarily "universal," but after the **formation** of the modern nation-state, Western-style masculinity has become mainstream worldwide. In other words, many people think that sportsman = masculine, but this is not true in Japan.

Indeed, looking back at previous Japanese films, Yuki Amami plays the role of Hikaru Genji in *A Thousand Years of Love: A Tale of Hikaru Genji*. In other words, the actress is playing the male role. The movie *Ooku* also depicts a world in which the genders have been reversed, and the main character, Yunoshin Mizuno（played by Kazuya Ninomiya）, was a cute general, a handsome man who would be adored by the ladies. It is based on such **depictions**, that Japan is said to be a feminine country. Japan is by no means a society where machismo **rules the roost**.

On the other hand, in the United States, as the term "anti-intellectualism" suggests, physical strength is valued more than **intellect**. American sports are typically baseball, football, basketball, and ice hockey. In fact, many movies also deal with these four sports, and football, in particular, is a symbolic American sport in the sense that it is an aggressive sport.

Many Japanese sports films make boys play sports normally associated with girls such as *Let's Go Jets*, which depicts cheerleading by boys, and *Water Boys*, which depicts synchronized swimming by boys. In the motif of *Water Boys*, *Dive* and *Grand Blue* show plenty of naked performances by "cute" young boys.

The issue I would like to address here is boxing. Boxing has a certain **unique** flavor among sports. First of all, the stereotype of boxing as a hungry sport still remains, and boxing is also a sport that exposes the naked body, but never, never a cute body, always a fighting body.

When we think of boxing movies, we remember *Rocky* as one of the most famous films of all time. *Rocky* was written and produced by Sylvester Stallone, who was still unknown at the time, and became a mega hit. The film was highly **acclaimed** and won the Academy Award for Best Picture and Best Director that year. What was most valuable about this film was that it

*Roman Empire：ローマ帝国。古代ローマの共和制の後から中世社会が始まるまでのおよそ1500年あまりの期間を指す。

*『大奥』：よしながふみ原作による江戸時代の日本を描いた作品。水野祐之進はこの作品の登場人物。

*anti-：反〜を表す接頭辞。しばしば接尾辞 -ism（〜主義）がつく語と結びつき、イデオロギーの対立などを表現する際に用いられる。

*cute：かわいらしい。一般的に子供っぽい、女性的という含みをもつ。

brightened up America at once, which until then had been dark and **somber** due to the aftereffects of the Vietnam War. It was a film that portrayed the Horatio Algeresque virtue that if people work hard, they will be rewarded. The main character is portrayed as weak-witted, but passionate about humanity and dedicated to hard work.

That said, according to professional boxers, there are no real boxers as muscular as Rocky. Boxing requires weight loss, and if you have that much muscle, you will weigh more, and as a result, you will be at a disadvantage in a fight because you will be forced to fight boxers who are better built than you as a result of pre-fight measurements. Rocky's body is only for the movie. He is intentionally made to look like a muscle man to suit American tastes.

Boxing, unlike football or baseball, is an individual sport. It can also be called a solitary sport. Martin Scorsese's *Raging Bull*, ranked among the AFI's top ten films of all time, is a masterpiece that approaches the **solitude** of human beings. It is not a sport in which a group of men work together to do their best. In the case of boxing, the protagonist is a lower-class person who is considered an "underdog," and is portrayed as having no other **path** to self-realization than boxing. It can be said that the boxer is a lone wolf who fights. Boxing is a fighting sport, and since men have always been regarded as the "fighting sex," the boxer is a kind of male archetype.

Boxers in the United States were originally of Irish descent, and they are often portrayed in films as poor physical laborers. Clint Eastwood's *Million Dollar Baby* is about a female boxer of Irish descent, who comes out of the country and works as a waitress, and there is a scene where she **sneaks** home leftover food from customers to eat herself.

Kimio Ito said that the "ouch!" is not something you see on TV, but is allowed in a movie. Well, when I think about it, I don't remember many TV dramas dealing with boxing. In the case of boxing, we see men fighting with their upper bodies naked, so perhaps it is too graphic to watch on TV. Television is **dripping**, but movies are something you have to be prepared to watch.

Mr. Ito also points out that boxing films are "imported to Japan from the US." Certainly, there are many films depicting boxing in Japan as well, but the **pioneering** boxing films were made in the 1950s and 1960s by Nikkatsu films, with actors such as Yujiro Ishihara. Yujiro was a man who dominated the world

*aftereffects：後遺症・余波。side-effect は副作用
*ホレイショ・アルジャー（1832-1899）：米国の小説家。努力によって貧困から富と成功を手に入れるアメリカンドリームを実現させる物語を生み出した。Algeresque でアルジャー的な。

*AFI：American Film Institute（米国映画協会）の略。米国映画協会

*archetype：[a:kitaip] と発音。

at the time with his uniquely Japanese physique and long legs. Yujiro, Tetsuya Watari, Keiichiro Akagi, Joe Shishido, and other tough guys with physiques far beyond the Japanese norm have played boxers. This trend continues to this day, with recent films such as Kenichi Matsuyama's *Blue*, Mirai Moriyama's *Underdog*, Eita's *Ringside Story*, and Masaki Suda's *Wilderness* being made **in succession**, but they are different from the original form of Japanese men.

In this context, I saw the live-action version of *Ashita no Joe* and thought it was a new trend. In the case of this movie, the original is a legendary manga, but the **poverty** of the original is gone. It is a metrosexual version, as if it were about a man who goes to a sports club. Rather than hungry boxing, it is a beautiful man boxing.

*physique：体格、体つき。physics や physician はそれぞれ全く別の意味を表すので注意。[fizi:k] と発音。

*metrosexual：ファッションや美容に強い関心をもつ男性のこと。metro は metropolitan（都会的な）の略。

EXERCISE ③ --

次の各文が、リーディングの内容と一致していれば T を、一致しなければ F を選び、〇をつけましょう。

	答え
① In the Heian and Tokugawa periods, low-class Japanese soldiers were defeated in a war against the European societies because of their lack of masculinity.	T ・ F
② Even now, in sports, physical strength is highly valued in the United States, whereas many Japanese sports have a cast of boys who play sports normally associated with girls.	T ・ F
③ The film *Rocky* describes a solemn period when American society had been struggling with the aftereffects of the Vietnam War.	T ・ F
④ Real boxers are usually less muscular than men like Rocky, because their heavy weight may be disadvantageous in a fight.	T ・ F
⑤ What makes boxing distinct from football and baseball is that boxing is an individual sport, so that there is neither a winner nor a loser in this sport.	T ・ F
⑥ Since boxers fight with their upper bodies naked, it is prohibited to make a TV drama dealing with boxing in the United States.	T ・ F
⑦ The live-action version of *Ashita no Joe* is considered to have opened the way for a new meterosexual trend, in which the story of a beautiful man boxing is screened.	T ・ F

⬤EXERCISE ④：Word Order --

文構造と文の意味を意識しながら、次の［　　］内の表現を並べ替えて、文法的にも意味的にも正しい文を作りましょう。

① Because of the disproportionate number of men in politics, [primarily by / decisions / men / made / are inevitably / war].

② There are differences in the basic abilities of men and women, both in power and speed, [is / are / by men and women / which / sports / played separately / why].

③ Gender stereotyping in [in American / sports / been / competition / a social phenomenon / society / has] for decades.

④ Feminine [a / sports / aesthetic / strong / component / have], while masculine sports emphasize strength and physical contact.

⑤ As for club activities at schools in Japan, [not / to / a few / or only boys / of them / join / allow / only girls], which means that there is a gender issue.

⑥ According to the Japan Boxing Commission, boxers are allowed to fight according to the sex on their family register, [gender / regardless / their / of / identity / own].

⑦ Countries [both sexes / eliminated / uphold / have / equal / that / rights for] gender-based restrictions in sports.

EXERCISE ⑤：Discussion／Writing ---

次の問いかけに関して、自分の考えをまとめてみましょう。

① In the 2020 Tokyo Olympics the German women's gymnastics team decided to wear "unitards," which cover the entire body instead of leotards. What are your thoughts on how sports should respond to gender diversity?

② What do you think about women participating in fighting sports, such as boxing, wrestling and sumo? Please state your views and explain why.

Chapter 07 Ikemen—Good-looking Men

美男美女は、文化を超えていつの時代も多くの人々にとって憧れです。イケメンの定義は文化によって様々といえるでしょうが、昨今では、日本でも男性がファッションや美容を楽しむようになっています。皆さんの周りには、イケメンはいますか？イケメンとは、あなたにとってどんな存在でしょう？イケメンであるためには顔だけでなく、身体を鍛えることも必要でしょうか？本章では、日本とアメリカのイケメンの定義について考えます。

PRE-EXERCISE

次の英語の映画タイトルから内容を推測しながら、語群の日本語タイトルと結びつけ、答えを書き入れましょう。

	答え		答え
① *Death Becomes Her*（1992）		④ *Emancipation*（2022）	
② *Shallow Hal*（2001）		⑤ *Triangle of Sadness*（2022）	
③ *Beauty and the Beast*（2017）		⑥ *Never Been Kissed*（1999）	

語群

a. 『逆転のトライアングル』　　　　b. 『美女と野獣』

c. 『25 年目のキス』　　　　　　　d. 『自由への道』

e. 『愛しのローズマリー』　　　　　f. 『永遠に美しく』

EXERCISE ①

次の文章はリーディング箇所で扱われている映画のあらすじです。文構造や文意を考えながら音声を聴いて、下線部に表現を書き入れてみましょう。

映画❶：『ハンサム★スーツ』（*The Handsome Suit*）

The Handsome Suit is a comedy movie about a man, Takuro who is (1)＿＿＿＿＿＿＿ but has an inferiority complex about his looks. One day he gets a suit that makes him handsome when he (2)＿＿＿＿＿＿＿ it. With this suit on, he becomes irresistibly appealing to women, becomes popular as a (3)＿＿＿＿＿＿＿, and seems to have found a happy life. Now, "what is more important (4)＿＿＿＿＿＿＿ life, appearance or substance?"

映画❷：『シラノ』（*Cyrano*）

> Cyrano, a brilliant knight with a talent for poetry as well as
> (1)＿＿＿＿＿＿, is unable to express his feelings for Roxanne he
> loves because he feels inferior in his (2)＿＿＿＿＿＿. Christian, a
> young man who had no talent for writing about his affections, also
> loved Roxanne. Despite Cyrano's true feelings, he writes a love letter
> to Roxanne (3)＿＿＿＿＿＿ Christian, (4)＿＿＿＿＿＿ his own
> feelings into words.

EXERCISE ②

次の英語表現と最も意味の近い日本語表現を語群から選び、答えを書き入れてみましょう。

	答え		答え		答え
① evaluate		⑥ in vogue		⑪ publicize	
② commit suicide		⑦ available		⑫ orient	
③ discrimination		⑧ perspective		⑬ enchant	
④ reinforce		⑨ obsess		⑭ self-gratification	
⑤ assessment		⑩ every once in a while		⑮ undergo	

語群

a. （変化などを）経る   b. 評価・査定   c. 方向づける
d. 差別   e. 評価する   f. 増長する・強化する
g. 流行して・人気があって   h. 必要以上に気にする   i. 自殺する
j. 利用できる・入手可能な   k. うっとりさせる   l. 自己満足
m. 視点・観点   n. 公表する   o. 時折・たまに

READING

The word "lookism" is seen frequently these days. It is a concept that **evaluates** people based on their beauty or ugliness of appearance and distinguishes between those who are physically attractive（beautiful men and women）and those who are not. It is also translated as "appearance supremacy".

A movie titled *Sakura* was released in 2020. In this movie, a young man, played by Ryo Yoshizawa, who had previously been handsome and popular, has an accident that scars his face and people around him stop approaching him. Despite the fact that his family loves him, he eventually **commits suicide**. It

*lookism：look（容姿）と -ism（主義）を合わせた造語。appearance supremacy（外見至上主義）ともいう。

was a shocking ending because the idea of a man killing himself over a facial scar was something unthinkable in past movies.

In the past, legal **discrimination** existed between women and men with regard to facial scars. Women were compensated more than men for injuries to the face due to accidents and other causes. Feminists were angry about that—they argued that it **reinforced** the stereotype that "a woman's face is important". On the men's side, perhaps many would consider it discrimination for them not to be compensated for their injuries because they are men.

*stereotype：多くの人に浸透している固定概念や思い込み

Laura Mulvey's (1975) theory of "Visual Pleasure and Narrative Cinema" is well known. In the past, it was more common for women than men to be represented as the sexual object seen in films. However, this is not necessarily the case any longer. It used to be said that "society's **assessment** of a man is not based on his looks", but now the world is changing to one in which appearance is important not only for women but also for men.

*Laura Mulvey：1941 年生まれのイギリスのフェミニスト映画理論家。現在は、ロンドン大学バークベック校の映画・メディア研究教授。
*Visual Pleasure and Narrative Cinema：「男・見る主体女・見られる客体」、1975 年のローラ・マルヴェイによる説。
*maternal instinct：母性本能
↔ paternal：父性

Japan is said to be a country inclined more to a feminine culture than Western countries. Even in the case of male actors, feminine men who tickle the maternal instinct, such as those who are called "Johnny's type" (stars represented by Johnny & Associates, Inc.), have been considered more popular in this country. These days, a gender-neutral face is said to be **in vogue**, and it has become common practice for men to keep their eyebrows in line, remove their beards and unwanted hair, apply emulsion and lotion, use sunscreen cream, and wax their hair. In fact, there are a number of men's esthetic salons nowadays. Many men go to gym, and hair removal and other services are also **available** at a lower cost than the past days, so the number of men who go to these services is increasing. Moreover, recently, some men have started to remove not only chest hair and leg hair, but also underarm hair and pubic hair.

This trend is progressive from a male gender **perspective** because it means that even men have the freedom to care about their appearances. The fact that people say that "a man's value is not in his looks" indicates, on the contrary, that "a man should not be concerned about the beauty or ugliness of his face". This is the opposite of the oppression that women feel from men. It has never been better for a man than to be good-looking. There have been movies with beautiful men as motifs, such as *The Handsome Suit* and *Boys Over Flowers*, but movies of this type were shown as comedies and turned the beautiful men into jokes. There was a general sense that it was unmanly

*Boys Over Flowers：神尾葉子による同名漫画「花より男子」の洋題。日本のみならずアニメ化、ドラマ化、映画化されている。

for a man to **obsess** over his facial beauty or body hair. A man with a complex about his appearance had no choice but to laugh at himself for it. For some of those who are involved, though, appearance complexes are a serious problem and are not a laughing matter at all.

It is not surprising that there are also movies in the United States in which ugly men suffer. An example of this is *Marty*. Although the movie was filmed 70 years ago, Ernest Borgnine, also known as Mr. Ugly, won the Academy Award for Best Actor in this movie, despite his ugliness. In the United States, the term "metrosexual" has come to describe urban men who go to gym, wear fashionable clothes, and go to the beauty parlor. **Every once in a while**, a ranking of the most beautiful men in America **publicized**, and many of America's top actors such as George Clooney, Brad Pitt, Johnny Depp and Matt Damon have a metrosexual image. On the other hand, in the U.S., there is an image of more muscular (macho) stars than in Japan. The United States is a country that was originally pioneered and built on unexplored lands, and has a tradition of demanding physical strength. The belief in macho still seems to be strong in the United States. Tarzan-like stars such as Jason Statham and Dwayne Johnson are still going strong. Statham and Johnson are both skinheads, and the hairstyle is a symbol of battle.

It seems that in the case of men in American movies, physique is more often an issue than facial beauty. Recently, a movie called *Cyrano* was released. Needless to say, this movie is based on *Cyrano de Bergerac*. The original story was about a man with a complex about his tall nose, but the movie adaptation of *Cyrano* uses a dwarf actor and the plot is **oriented** around his short stature. *Shallow Hal* is another comedy about a romance between a short man and a tall woman. This movie also shows that the idea that men should be taller than women remains strong-rooted even now.

However, it is not by all means the case that women are attracted to macho men. It is a common theory that men who are the protagonists of romantic movies are feminized, and the plot involves men who are sensitive and romantic falling in love with women. The proof is that muscle stars like Statham and Johnson seldom appear in love affairs with women. Even in the movie *Cyrano*, the protagonist, who is not confident in his appearance writes honeyed phrases to a woman for another man. The woman is completely **enchanted** by these poetic lines. Thus, this implies that men in love are

*Ernest Borgnine：（1917-2012）米国俳優。生涯で200本近くの作品に出演している。
*metrosexual：外見や生活様式への強い美意識を持つ男性のこと

*Dwayne Johnson：米国俳優。元プロレスラー
*go strong：根強い人気である。go ＋形容詞は「〜の状態になる」。
*physique：（特に男性の）体格。フランス語が語源。アクセントが後ろにあるので注意。
*Cyrano de Bergerac：『シラノ・ド・ベルジュラック』はエドモン・ロスタン作の韻文戯曲。17世紀フランスに実在した剣豪作家を主人公にした作品。
*protagonist：主人公、主役

somewhat feminine.

According to the book, *The Adonis Complex*, some data show that women prefer a normal body better than men think. It may be said that muscle is a man's **self-gratification**. In Japan, the word "*hoso-macho*" has become popular. It means that the body is trained in a masculine way, but the muscles are not built too big to oppress women. These men also try to remove the elements that women dislike, such as sweat, odor, and hair. In short, the struggle between masculinity and femininity can be seen in the bodies of men.

Although the basic idea is that the U.S. seeks macho men, and Japan seeks cute ones, both countries are **undergoing** the same transformation for men to be conscious of themselves as "objects to be looked at" in this age. That men have also been given the right to look beautiful could deserve positive recognition.

The Adonis Complex：ハーバード・メディカル精神科教授であるHarrison. G. Pope によ る 著 書。男性の肉体美・肉体強化への執着をテーマにした本。

EXERCISE ③ --

次の各文が、リーディングの内容と一致していれば T を、一致しなければ F を選び、〇をつけましょう。

	答え
① In the past, men were compensated more than women for facial injuries caused by accidents.	T・F
② According to the writer, the tendency today is that appearance is highly regarded not only for women but also men.	T・F
③ Nowadays, while many men go to esthetic salons, fewer men are going to the gym.	T・F
④ This essay says some films that use beautiful men as a motif have turned them into a laughing matter.	T・F
⑤ Compared with Japan, there are more macho stars in the United States.	T・F
⑥ The original story of the film, *Cyrano* is based on a woman who has a complex about her height.	T・F
⑦ The term "*hoso-macho*" is popular in the United States, but not in Japan on the contrary.	T・F

文構造と文の意味を意識しながら、次の［　　］内の表現を並べ替えて、文法的にも意味的にも正しい文を作りましょう。

---

① The word "lookism" refers [based on / are / to / evaluated / the idea / that / the beauty or ugliness / people] of their appearance, and is sometimes translated as "appearance supremacy".

---

② Japan is said [the West / than / a more feminine culture / to / those of / be], and men tickle the maternal instinct are more popular.

---

③ These days, [more and more / it / even men / seems / that / obvious / to be / apply] emulsion, lotion, and sunscreen cream.

---

④ The United States is a country built on unexplored land, and [men / expected / to be / there is / that / physically / a tradition / strong / have been].

---

⑤ In romance movies, [the plot / a man / often / who / is attentive to / revolves / around / details] and romantically sensitive, and that type of man falls in love with a woman.

---

⑥ Some date suggest [women / prefer / that / normal bodies / muscles / to excessively-well-built], and that a muscular figure may be for a man's self-gratification.

---

⑦ In both Japan and the U.S., [a growing trend / among / there is / more concerned / their appearance / men / to be / about].

EXERCISE ⑤：Discussion／Writing

次の問いかけに関して、自分の考えをまとめてみましょう。

① Please note the following statement in the text; it has become common practice for men to keep their eyebrows in line, remove their beards and unwanted hair, apply emulsion and lotion, use sunscreen cream, and wax their hair. What do you think about this tendency among men?

② Do you think there is still a tendency for men to be taller than women, as seen in the film *Shallow Hal* mentioned in the text?

Chapter 08 Artists

皆さんは、芸術家といえば、どんな印象を抱いているでしょうか。音楽家を想像する人もいれば、画家を想像する人もいますね。芸術家と言っても芸術を生業としているプロもいるでしょうし、芸術を愛するアマチュアもいるでしょう。皆さんは、芸術家に女性的なイメージを持っていますか、または、男性的なイメージを持っていますか。芸術家に対するイメージを膨らませながら、本章の学習を進めていきましょう。

PRE-EXERCISE

次の英語の映画タイトルから内容を推測しながら、語群の日本語タイトルと結びつけ、答えを書き入れましょう。

	答え		答え
① *Lust for Life*（1956）		④ *Begin Again*（2013）	
② *Girl with a Pearl Earring*（2003）		⑤ *At Eternity's Gate*（2018）	
③ *The Happy Prince*（2018）		⑥ *As Good as It Gets*（1997）	

語群

a. 『真珠の耳飾りの少女』　　　　　b. 『永遠の門 ゴッホの見た未来』

c. 『さすらいの人 オスカー・ワイルド』　d. 『恋愛小説家』

e. 『はじまりのうた』　　　　　　　f. 『炎の人ゴッホ』

EXERCISE ①

次の文章はリーディング箇所で扱われている映画のあらすじです。文構造や文意を考えながら音声を聴いて、下線部に表現を書き入れてみましょう。

映画❶：『パターソン』（*Paterson*）

Paterson, a bus driver living in Paterson, New Jersey, makes it a
（1）＿＿＿＿＿＿ to write down in a notebook what has been
（2）＿＿＿＿＿＿ in his mind as a poem in between bus rides.
The film （3）＿＿＿＿＿ Paterson's seven-day routine: waking
up in the morning with a kiss for his wife Laura, heading to work,
（4）＿＿＿＿＿ his bus driver's ride, coming home to have dinner
with his wife, and having a drink at the bar on his way to walk his dog.

映画❷：『永い言い訳』（*The Long Excuse*）

> Yukio Kinugasa, a popular writer, learns that his wife had an (1) _____ on a trip and died along with his best friend. Yukio, who had no love for his wife and had been having an (2) _____ with someone else, is unable to (3) _____ for her death. Yukio meets Yoichi Omiya, the (4) _____ son of his wife's best friend, and their two children. Yukio begins to take care of Yoichi's children. Yukio begins to devote himself to the Omiya family.

EXERCISE ② --

次の英語表現と最も意味の近い日本語表現を語群から選び、答えを書き入れてみましょう。

	答え		答え		答え
① subtle		⑥ bullied		⑪ make a living	
② overwhelmingly		⑦ combative		⑫ marital relationship	
③ pioneering		⑧ masculine		⑬ protagonist	
④ feminine		⑨ glean		⑭ dismal	
⑤ occupied		⑩ redemption		⑮ assert	

 語群

a. 圧倒的に	b. 主張する	c. 闘争的な
d. 夫婦関係	e. 微妙な	f. 生計を立てる
g. 汲み取る	h. 悲惨な	i. 先駆的な
j. 女性的な	k. 男性的な	l. 贖罪
m. 主人公	n. 忙しい	o. いじめられる

READING --

The profession of artist is a subtle one when considered from the perspective of masculinity. It is overwhelmingly men who have produced the greatest art, music, literature, theater, etc. throughout human history, but that does not mean that the artist is a masculine profession.

There is a pioneering film about male gender issues called *Tea and Sympathy*. The film is set in a high school boys' dormitory and depicts the heart-to-heart relationship between Tom, a boy who is bullied for being a feminine boy, and Laura, the housemaster's wife, who tries to protect him.

*from the perspective of masculinity： 男性性（男らしさ）の観点から。

*housemaster：舎監（寄宿舎を管理している教師のこと。）

Tom is a young man who shows an interest in theater and music, which seems feminine to other athletic, muscle-bound boys, and because of this he is bullied as a "sister boy" (a boy like his sisters). The arts, such as music, literature, etc., are seen as appealing to the emotions and rather feminine. The stereotype of men as combative and women as emotional has always existed.

Professions of art and beauty, such as hairdressers and designers, are the domain of homosexual and androgenous men, and in many cases they are still the stereotypical occupations of gay people. In fact, many men who left great works of art, such as Michelangelo and Oscar Wilde, were gay.

Therefore, if you want to portray a heterosexual male with an artistic-character in a film, you have to include a masculine element to that character somewhere.

There is a movie called *The Long Excuse* about a novelist who loses his wife in an accident. In the first scene, we see him getting a haircut from his wife. What can be gleaned from their conversation at this point is that his wife supported him financially during "the time when he could not feed himself." Many artists are financially dependent on women in their lives because they have a long road toward making a living from their art.

In Japan, it is clear that the idea of women backing up their husbands' work is still very strong. According to Kimio Ito, in Japan, "the rules of the marital relationship are more ambiguous" than in the West. Furthermore, "the type of system in which women support men who are not capable of making a living is stronger." It is true that in Japan today, there are many families in which both parents have to work to make a living, and the wife is the main income earner, but in the case of Japanese women, there are still many women who work to support their husbands and families, rather than working for self-reliance and self-realization. I believe that there are still many women who work to support their husbands and families. As the scene of a man having his hair cut by a woman suggests, the woman is the one who takes care of the man, and the man is the one who is taken care of.

After the scene of the haircut in *The Long Excuse*, the wife dies in an accident, but the novelist was actually with his mistress at the time of her accident. In the past, it was said that "cheating is a man's prerogative," and this also confirms the masculine gender of the protagonist. After his wife's death, his

*muscle-bound boys：筋肉マッチョの男子。

*androgenous men: 両性具有的（男女両性を備えている）男子。

*self-reliance：自立
*self-realization： 自己実現

*"cheating is a man's prerogative"：「浮気は男の甲斐性。」（妻も愛人も養えるだけの財力や包容力がある男性は、浮気をしても許されるという意味。）cheating：浮気
*prerogative：（地位によって与えられる）特権

room is a dismal mess, which also symbolize the male gender. The fact that he gets drunk and gets involved with his publisher symbolizes the male gender as well. There are no explicitly masculine moments, but these characteristics clearly portray that he is a male gendered person.

The film shows how he gradually develops his feminine side by taking care of his friend's children, who are being raised by a man. It is not much fun for a woman to do the same thing he is struggling to do to raise the children. It is common for women to be occupied with their children, so there is no drama.

Later in the film, he preaches to the child, "You cry not because you are weak. Strong people are sad and cry properly." Generally, we grow up being told that "boys shouldn't cry," but this line rejects the male gender stereotype, saying that this idea is wrong. He also develops an appreciation for women as a result of his wife's death. It can be seen as a story of redemption for a man who cheated on his wife and gave her trouble.

Thus, even though it depicts an artist, it is basically a story about a masculine man who changes into a feminine man in some aspect.

How about in the United States? There is a movie called *Paterson*. This is the story of just a week in the routine of a bus driver in the town of Paterson. He is a poet and keeps a notebook with poems he has written, but he never tries to market himself as a poet.

As the title *Paterson* suggests, the main character of the film is the town of Paterson, and the theme is the daily life of a man who lives there quietly. It is a world where, as one site（https://reasonandmeaning.com/2018/02/14/meaning-of-the-movie-paterson/）analyzes, "toxic masculinity and oversexualized femininity do not emerge."

His wife is the kind of woman who finds pleasure in turning everyday life into an art form, from playing guitar to baking cakes to painting the walls of their house. Paterson gently observes her as she does so. They do not fight with each other or selfishly assert themselves, but rather the film depicts their days passing by in a casual manner. Neither Paterson nor his wife seem to be gender-obsessed, but they are subtly at odds with each other, reminding me of the famous book *Men Are from Mars, Women Are from Venus: The Classic Guide to Understanding the Opposite Sex*.

*toxic masculinity：有害な男らしさ。（男は強くあるべきと言われて育った男性が暴力やDVに走ってしまうなど男らしさの負の側面のこと。）
*oversexualized femininity：過剰に性的に表現された女性性。

The only thing that is gendered in this film is, dare I say it, that the main character's occupation is that of a driver, a habitually male occupation. But there are many female bus drivers in the U.S. nowadays.

This is a work that will make us think about the future of male-female relationships. From now on, not only macho masculinity but also artist masculinity will be studied.

EXERCISE ③ --

次の各文が、リーディングの内容と一致していれば T を、一致しなければ F を選び、○をつけましょう。

	答え
① According to the author, the artist is a masculine profession because the greatest artists, musicians, writers are mostly men.	T ・ F
② In the film, *Tea and Sympathy*, the boy is called "sister boy" because he likes his sisters.	T ・ F
③ The author argues that hairdressers and designers are the stereotypical professions of men who are homosexual and bisexual.	T ・ F
④ According to the author, the novelist's wife in the film, *The Long Excuse*, supported her husband financially until he became successful as a novelist.	T ・ F
⑤ In the film, *The Long Excuse*, the novelists who was a male gendered person has become a feminine man as he takes care of his friend's children.	T ・ F
⑥ The film, *Paterson*, describes how the main character became successful as a poet.	T ・ F
⑦ The main character of *Paterson* is supported financially by his wife.	T ・ F

EXERCISE ④ ： Word Order --

文構造と文の意味を意識しながら、次の [　　] 内の表現を並べ替えて、文法的にも意味的にも正しい文を作りましょう。

① Oscar Wilde is an Irish writer [was /playwright / 1854 / and / born / who / in], and *The Picture of Dorian Gray* is the most familiar of his works.

② One of Japan's [which / art / islands / Naoshima / is / located / is / in] the Seto Inland Sea. You can see famous pumpkin art work created by Kusama Yayoi there.

③ Some professions such as nurse and flight attendant used to be professions for women; however, those [become /for /professions / as / common / men / have / well].

④ Kimio Ito is [whose / gender / sociologist / research / a / specialization / is] and culture from a masculinities perspective.

⑤ In the past, most Takarazuka Revue fans were women, but recently [has / the / increasing / male / number/ been / of / fans].

⑥ Masatoshi Nagase plays a Japanese poet in a film called *Paterson*, and at the end of the film, [converses/ character / he / and / the / meets / main / with], Paterson.

⑦ The play called *Our Town*, written by Thornton Wilder, depicts [lives / in / everyday / live / of / people / the / who] a small town in America.

EXERCISE ⑤：Discussion／Writing

次の問いかけに関して、自分の考えをまとめてみましょう。

① For women: Would you like to support your husband financially until he becomes successful? What if your husband were an artist who could not feed himself?
For men: Would you like to be supported by your wife if you were an artist who could not feed yourself? Please explain your opinion along with your reasons.

② The author states that "it is overwhelmingly men who have produced the greatest art, music, literature, theater, etc. throughout human history." Why do you think that it is overwhelmingly men who have been the greatest artists?

Chapter 09 Otaku

「オタク」と聞くと、どんなイメージを持っていますか？あなたは自分をオタクだと思いますか？ 1980 年代に日本のサブカルチャーから広まったこの言葉は、当初はマイナスなイメージが強かったのですが、今では、単純に何かに熱中している人や、一つのことに没頭している人のことを指し、プラスのイメージへと変わってきています。時代と共にオタクの意味も定義も変化しているのです。英語では、geek・nerd・freak など、オタクを指す言葉にはいくつかの種類があります。本章では、日本とアメリカの「オタク」のイメージについて考えてみましょう。

ⓅRE-EXERCISE

次の英語の映画タイトルから内容を推測しながら、語群の日本語タイトルと結びつけ、答えを書き入れましょう。

	答え		答え
① *Role Models*（2008）		④ *Blood Fest*（2018）	
② *Hidden Figures*（2016）		⑤ *Office Space*（1999）	
③ *Almost Famous*（2000）		⑥ *The Mummy*（1999）	

語群

a. 『ドリーム』　　　　　　　　　b. 『ぼくたちの奉仕活動』
c. 『リストラ・マン』　　　　　　d. 『モンスター・フェスティバル』
e. 『あの頃ペニー・レインと』　　f. 『ハムナプトラ / 失われた砂漠の都』

ⒺXERCISE ①

次の文章はリーディング箇所で扱われている映画のあらすじです。文構造や文意を考えながら音声を聴いて、下線部に表現を書き入れてみましょう。

映画❶：『ヲタクに恋は難しい』（*Wotakoi: Love Is Hard for Otaku*）

A 26-year-old, Narumi Momose, meets her（1）_____ friend, Hirotaka Nito, again at her new job. Hirotaka, who is good-looking and good at his job, is a（2）_____ video game *otaku*. Narumi is also an *otaku* who loves manga, games, and cosplay. The only time Narumi can（3）_____ her true self is in front of her *otaku* friend Hirotaka. The two *otaku* started to go out（4）_____....

映画❷：『ソーシャル・ネットワーク』（*The Social Network*）

> This movie is about the life of Mark Zuckerberg, a (1)＿＿＿＿＿＿＿＿
> of the world's largest social networking site, Facebook. 19-year-
> old Harvard student Mark and his best friend (2)＿＿＿＿＿＿＿＿ a
> networking service in 2003 to help people make friends on campus.
> The service quickly became (3)＿＿＿＿＿＿＿＿ at other schools and
> grew into a huge site that became a social (4)＿＿＿＿＿＿＿＿.

ⒺXERCISE ②

次の英語表現と最も意味の近い日本語表現を語群から選び、答えを書き入れてみましょう。

	答え		答え		答え
① variant		⑥ disorder		⑪ dichotomy	
② self-sufficient		⑦ deliberately		⑫ derive	
③ absorbed		⑧ discriminatory		⑬ fierce	
④ withdrawn		⑨ scatterbrained		⑭ indeed	
⑤ disability		⑩ struggle		⑮ fellow	

語群

a. わざと・意図的に	b. 夢中の・はまった	c. 自己充足的な
d. 障がい	e. 差別的な	f. 二分・両分
g. 〜の由来をたどる	h. 激しい・猛烈な	i. 奮闘する
j. 確かに・本当に	k. 引きこもった	l. 仲間・同志
m. 変異体・異型	n. 注意散漫な	o. 疾患・病気

ⓇEADING

There is a book titled *The Failed Men*, which talks about how men are the
"failed" sex. The argument in the book is that the fundamental form of human
beings is female. Males are a **variant**. It is said that women confirm that they
are women in a natural way because of menstruation and childbirth. Men,
on the other hand, are the constructed sex. Therefore, men are said to have a
fragile gender self-awareness, and thus their male identity wavers if they are
not constantly doing masculine things.

Women are **self-sufficient**, like Da Vinci's Mona Lisa sitting with smile on her
face. That is the archetype of a woman. Woman is a microcosm. Women have

*The Failed Men：原
作は『できそこな
いの男たち』2008
年、福岡神の著書。

XX chromosomes and men have XY chromosomes. Therefore, it is said that men are unbalanced and can only do one thing at a time.

This is why people say that all men are *otaku*. In general, men tend to be more **absorbed** in one thing. For example, when it comes to cooking, women can make delicious meals with ingredients they have on hand, but men who love to cook are likely to order specific ingredients and want to do things like professionals, which is also uneconomical.

It is said that men are more likely to be truant, **withdrawn**, or have developmental or learning **disabilities** because they tend to use their energy on one interest. However, it has been found lately that people with outstanding talents, such as Edison and Einstein, are rather more likely to have Asperger and other **disorders**. This is because it is possible to say that they achieved greatness because they focused on one thing.

Although *otaku* can be considered the most masculine, they are often portrayed as dowdy and rarely portrayed as good-looking in movies.

Takayuki Yamada is a good-looking man, but in the movie *Train Man* he **deliberately** transformed himself into a shabby man. Ryan Gosling also intentionally gained weight in *Lars and the Real Girl* and removed the aura of a handsome man. This may be a prejudice, but rather it would have been more interesting if he had kept his cool look.

In American movies, *otaku* are also computer geeks, and excellent films have been made about them, including *The Social Network*, about Facebook founder Mark Zuckerberg, and *Steve Jobs*, about Apple founder Steve Jobs. Older films, such as *War Games*, featured a video game *otaku*, played by Matthew Broderick. He is very small for an American. The main character in *Back to the Future* is also categorized as an *otaku*, and Michael J. Fox is also small.

Thus, the person who is good-looking, fit, and cool will not be cast in the role of *otaku*. This may be that *otaku* don't care about their appearance because they focus their attention only on their interests, and they don't care much about romance, but this is still a stereotype and a **discriminatory** view.

Another problem is that many of the *otaku* movies are comedies. There was a movie in the 1980s called *Revenge of the Nerds*, which is a story about nerds

*chromosome：染色体。46本ある染色体の44本が常染色体で、残りの2本が性染色体と呼ばれ、これにより性が決定する。
*otaku：自分の好きな事柄や興味のある分野、特にサブカルチャーに傾倒し、詳しい知識をもっている人のこと。
*truant：無断欠席の、ずる休みしている

*Asperger (Syndrome)：広汎性発達障害の一種。知的障害や言語障害を伴わない自閉症の症状をさす。
*dowdy：さえない、野暮ったい

*shabby：みすぼらしい服装の

*geek：もともと、さえない人や変わり者といったネガティブな意味であったが、インターネットの普及によりIT企業のCEOたちがロールモデルとなり、コンピューターの専門家のようなポジティブな意味にも使われるように変化してきた。

*nerd：日本語のオタクに近い意味をもつ。ある物事に強い興味を持ち、それに関する知識が豊富であるが、流行に疎く、外見的に魅力のない人をいう。

being exploited by macho bullies. While their revenge is achieved, there was still a sense that the movie made fun of *otaku*.

At the time, a book titled *The Peter Pan Syndrome: Men Who Have Never Grown Up* was published. The author, Dan Kiley, analyzes the male psychology in the book and states that the scenario for boys is to be either a comedian, a macho man, or a homosexual. In other words, there are only three possible scenarios for a man: macho, gay, or **scatterbrained**, which is, playing the clown and laughing at himself.

*homosexual：（名詞）同性愛者

Therefore, sensitive, non-macho, heterosexual boys have no choice but to laugh at themselves. However, there are more boys who are seriously **struggling** and can't laugh at themselves. We need more options for male scenarios to solve male problems.

*heterosexual：（形容詞）異性愛の

The stereotype that *otaku* are not popular is strong, but in Japan, Love Supremacism is a recently introduced concept. It must have been around 1970 that love marriages exceeded arranged marriages in Japan. Until then, the majority of people were married through arranged marriages to partners decided by their parents. With this in mind, it would be a mistake to put too much emphasis on Love Supremacism.

*Love Supremacism：恋愛至上主義。人生において恋愛を最も価値のあるものであると考える思想。

It is believed that there is now a **dichotomy** between those who date and those who do not, and the option of not dating the opposite sex is a great step forward.

Comparing Japanese and American *otaku* males in movies, American *otaku* are often portrayed as the brainy type, and in addition to the movies mentioned above, *Ready Player One* is another example. It is a story about dominating a virtual reality world and is **derived** from *The Matrix* and *Avatar*. When you can transform yourself into a cool avatar, *otaku* have a new option. The scale of the U.S. is huge, and competition is **fierce** because they want to rule the world with their avatars. It reminds us that the U.S. is a masculine country in the traditional sense. The U.S. is **indeed** a macho country, and there are a lot of stories about computer and game *otaku*, and how *otaku* will rule the world.

*Ready Player One：2011 年に上映された映画で Ernest Cline の小説がもとになっている。
*avatar：アバター。化身。インターネットなどの仮想空間において、自分の分身として表示されるキャラクターのこと。

On the other hand, Japanese *otaku* movies, such as *In Those Days*, about a rock band and *Watakoi: Love Is Hard for Otaku*, are rather cute *otaku*. The lead actors, Tori Matsuzaka and Naoto Fujiwara, are cute *otaku* who would be accepted by girls, even though they dress uncouthly and wear square glasses

*uncouthly：野暮に、無骨に

to mask their good-looking smiles. In Japan, for some reason, there are few stories about computer *otaku* and game *otaku*, and many stories are about anime *otaku* such as *Anime Supremacy*.

It is not wrong to think of Japan as feminine and the U.S. as masculine. It seems that even among the same *otaku*, the U.S. is more political and larger in scale, while Japan is often portrayed as a place where it is enough to be accepted only by **fellow** *otaku*.

EXERCISE ③

次の各文が、リーディングの内容と一致していれば T を、一致しなければ F を選び、〇をつけましょう。

	答え
① It is said that women are well-balanced and more self-sufficient than men.	T・F
② Tall good-looking men are often cast as nerds in many American movies.	T・F
③ According to the writer, it is a stereotype to believe that *otaku* only focus on their interests and are not so interested in love romance.	T・F
④ In both Japanese and American *otaku* movies, *otaku* are often portrayed as the brainy type.	T・F
⑤ You can find many Japanese *otaku* movies about computer geeks.	T・F
⑥ The writer thinks it is a problem that most of the *otaku* movies are comedies which make fun of the *otaku* characters in their stories.	T・F
⑦ The writer believes that the media presentation of two cultures, Japan as feminine and the U.S. as masculine, is unacceptable.	T・F

EXERCISE ④ : Word Order

文構造と文の意味を意識しながら、次の［　］内の表現を並べ替えて、文法的にも意味的にも正しい文を作りましょう。

① Akihabara, [is / a mecca / from Japan / which / for *otaku* / abroad / and / now called], was once internationally famous as the world's largest electronics town and was crowded not only with Japanese but also with foreign tourists.

② According to a survey by a research institute, one out of five young people is already an *otaku*, and [grow / this ratio / three / is / one / to / expected to / out of] by 2030.

③ Marketers used to target *otaku* who were interested in specific genres such as animation, games, and railroads, but recently [experts in / their marketing / have / who / expanded / to / people / they / are] cosmetics, beauty products, and 100-yen stores.

④ Because *otaku* [like / are /about / they / the things / purchasing / very enthusiastic], more and more companies are approaching the *otaku* market in many ways.

⑤ Nowadays, as many social networking sites have developed, [ordinary people / have / for / it / knowledge / is / not unusual / to] that is as deep as that of professionals in the field.

⑥ Contents tourism, which promotes [to / that / appeared / have / pilgrimages / in / places and buildings] animations and movies, is in high demand from inbound travelers.

⑦ COOL JAPAN is [that / policy / aims / increase / an economic / market value / to / Japanese] leading to nation-wide economic growth by actively presenting Japan's attractiveness from the perspective of foreign visitors.

EXERCISE ⑤ : Discussion／Writing --

> 次の問いかけに関して、自分の考えをまとめてみましょう。

① When you hear the word *otaku*, what image do you have of them? Please explain your thoughts along with your reasons.

② Recently, the word *otaku* is used to describe a person who knows a great deal about a particular subject. Do you consider yourself *otaku*? Why or why not?

Chapter 10 Incel

アメリカの SNS 上などで、自分を「インセル」だと名乗る男達のコミュニティが最近注目を集めています。自分が女性とうまくいかないのは女性側のせいだと彼らは考えているようです。インセルは主に白人男性で、社会では性別的にも人種的にも優位にあるはずなのに、男女平等や人種差別撤廃を求められるせいで不当にも虐げられている、と感じているのです。その劣等感や憂さを晴らすために攻撃的な言動に走り、その結果、暴力的であればあるほど仲間内での評価が高まるという歪な状況が生まれ、凄惨な事件を引き起こすことさえあるのです。このインセルのムーブメントはアメリカに留まらず、世界に広がりを見せています。

ⓟ PRE-EXERCISE

次の英語の映画タイトルから内容を推測しながら、語群の日本語タイトルと結びつけ、答えを書き入れましょう。

	答え		答え
① *Revenge of the Nerds*（1984）		④ *Heavy*（1995）	
② *Alone with Her*（2006）		⑤ *What Women Want*（2000）	
③ *To Kill a Mockingbird*（1962）		⑥ *her*（2013）	

語群

a.『君に逢いたくて』　　　　　　　b.『アラバマ物語』

c.『ハート・オブ・ウーマン』　　　d.『世界でひとつの彼女』

e.『集結！恐怖のオチコボレ軍団』　f.『覗かれる女』

ⓔ EXERCISE ①

次の文章はリーディング箇所で扱われている映画のあらすじです。文構造や文意を考えながら音声を聴いて、下線部に表現を書き入れてみましょう。

映画❶：『悪人』（*Villain*）

Shimizu Yuichi, a（1）＿＿＿＿＿＿＿, lives a lonely life while taking care of his grandparents. He never knows what is like to be loved and kills a woman he met on a（2）＿＿＿＿＿＿. He becomes the（3）＿＿＿＿＿ that has been in the news every day, and goes on a（4）＿＿＿＿＿ escape with a lonely woman, Mitsuyo. How did Yuichi come to kill a woman? Who is the real "villain"?

映画❷：『ジョーカー』(*Joker*)

> Arthur Fleck, a (1)＿＿＿＿＿＿＿＿ man, lives with his sickly mother
> in a corner of the (2)＿＿＿＿＿＿＿＿ big city. He dreams of success
> as a comedian, but for a living, he puts on clown's makeup and works
> as a street performer. While living humbly, he is (3)＿＿＿＿＿＿＿
> attacked by a gang of thugs. (4)＿＿＿＿＿＿＿ by society, Arthur
> gradually becomes obsessed with madness and then transforms into
> a charismatic criminal named Joker.

❶EXERCISE ② --

次の英語表現と最も意味の近い日本語表現を語群から選び、答えを書き入れてみましょう。

	答え		答え		答え
① resentment		⑥ aggressive		⑪ disgusting	
② accusation		⑦ adopt		⑫ anguish	
③ misogyny		⑧ ignite		⑬ victimize	
④ degrade		⑨ condemn		⑭ abuse	
⑤ confidence		⑩ commit		⑮ diversity	

語群

a. 多様性	b. 火をつける	c. 女性蔑視
d. 非難	e. 品位を落とす	f. 攻撃的な
g. （罪を）犯す	h. 虐待	i. 気持ち悪い
j. 自信	k. 恨み	l. （人を）不当に苦しめる
m. 苦悩	n. 非難する	o. 養子にする

❶READING --

Recently, the term "incel," short for involuntary celibates, has been
popularized in the United States. Incel refers to a community of men who,
despite their desire, are unable to have romantic or sexual relationships with
women and believe that the problem lies not with themselves but with their
partners. They become misogynists out of **resentment** over their inability to
have relationships with women, and sometimes launch violent attacks and
accusations against women.

However, **misogyny** is not what started recently; rather, it is the general

*misogyny: 言葉とし
ての起源は 17 世紀
に遡る。

concept. The theory of homosociality, developed in Eve Sedgwick's *Between Men: English Literature and Male Homosocial Desire*, which had a major impact on academia, defined misogyny as referring to relationships between men that encompass homophobia. In other words, those who live in a homosocial world hate homosexuality and have to make women the object of their sexual desires, while at the same time having a certain misogynistic side.

In particular, American films are considered to be originally misogynistic. The book *America on Film* introduced the term "hegemonic negotiation" and argues that even in the feminist era, when American films may portray women as seemingly stronger, they ultimately have an aspect of **degrading** women.

On the other hand, incels, which have emerged in the 21st century, are a more **aggressive** group of women-haters, who try to express their anger in an anti-social way. More recently, there is even a specific online movement called MGTOW (Men Going Their Own Way), whose members hostilely refuse to date or have sexual relations with women from the outset.

Joker is a classic example of an American film that deals with the case of incel. Arthur Fleck, the protagonist of this story, who later becomes Joker, works as a clown and suffers from Pseudobulbar Affect (PBA), which causes him to laugh and cry violently and suddenly.

He has seen a counselor but shows no signs of recovery; he does not date women, has no friends, and lives alone with his mother, who suffers from a delusional mental disorder.

He searches for his father, whom he has never met, but eventually discovers that he is in fact a child **adopted** by his mother, that he is not related to her and that he does not know who his father is either. This revelation **ignites** his unstable mind and he kills his mother and goes on to **commit** a series of other murders.

Although he becomes a serial killer, the film does not completely **condemn** him as a criminal. Rather, the focus is on his mind. He is an incel, the type of man that women find **disgusting**, yet his inescapable **anguish** is depicted.

More recently, the term "black pill" has been introduced: it means ① women control men by manipulating their sexual desires. ② Women base their relationships on men's appearance and social status, and women have the

*homosociality：ホモソーシャル。男性間の緊密な結びつきを意味する社会学の用語。

*イヴ・セジウィック（1950-2009）：アメリカのホモソーシャル論の第一人者。Chapter 1 の注にて詳述。

*hegemonic negotiation：覇権調整。伝統的な男社会においては覇権的男性性（hegemonic masculinity）が支配権を握る要素とされてきた。しかし男女平等社会を目指す中、女性も覇権闘争に参画する存在であると認識され、覇権の調整が行われているとする用語。

*MGTOW：ミグタウ。「我が道を行く男性たち」の意。恋愛や結婚が非効率的であるとする男性たち。

*Joker：DC コミックの『バットマン』シリーズが生み出したカリスマ的悪役。本作品（2019）において、ジョーカー役を演じたホアキン・フェニックスが第 92 回アカデミー主演男優賞を獲得した。

*a serial killer：異常な心理的欲求のもと、一定の冷却期間をおきながらも長期間にわたって複数の殺人を繰り返す連続殺人犯のこと。

choice whether or not to fall in love. ③ There is a biological basis for this. According to those who have taken the "black pill," they wake up to the truth shown above.

(https://note.com/outside_suicide/n/n80457f1e5a49)

In Japan, groups that could be regarded as incels have not appeared as yet. However, we are gradually seeing stories of men being **victimized** by women in the movies.

The first thing to note is the award-winning film *Villain*. Yuichi, the protagonist in this movie, has been traumatized by neglect from his mother, has low self-esteem, and can only date women he meets on dating sites. One day, he unintentionally kills Yoshino, whom he met on the online dating site. He loses himself owing to her attempts to not only demand money from him, but also to frame him as the perpetrator of the rape.

In *Birds Without Names*, the protagonist's（Sadao Abe）wife, played by Yu Aoi, is a selfish and unfaithful woman. She constantly hurls cruel words at her husband, gouging his heart; it is indeed verbal abuse. But he is undaunted, continues to love her, and takes care of the rest of her life so that he can live his own life. He is a pathetic man, but this is because he has no **confidence** in his own attractiveness as a man. The film is full of the pathos of a husband who never wins against his wife.

The protagonist in *Villain* has a certain hatred towards women because he believes he is not worthy of being loved, while the protagonist in *Birds Without Names* can only flatter women and is self-destructive. Do people who have never been loved or have been abused have to come to a sad end? Even if they commit crimes, men will never be saved if we do not consider the issues behind it.

The time has come to consider the damage given to men as well.

As an aside, in *The Disease Called Capital Punishment*, Sadao Abe plays the role of a serial killer with an overwhelming presence. The story traces the memory of upbringing of the protagonist, played by Kenshi Okada, as he interacts with the serial killer who has been sentenced to death. Audiences will find the story too dark, too heavy and unnecessarily awful to bear, but a range of contemporary issues are covered. It is a story of suffering that only people who have been **abused** can understand.

*black pill：インセルの仲間内だけで通じる用語であり、「インセルに覚醒する」という意味を持つ。映画『マトリックス』にインスパイアされたアンチ・フェミニストが用いる「レッド・ピルを飲む」に由来する。

*Villain：『悪人』（2010）。李相日監督作品。妻夫木聡主演。吉田修一原作。

*Birds Without Names：『彼女がその名を知らない鳥たち』（2017）。『凶悪』、『日本で一番悪い奴ら』の白石和彌監督作品。沼田まほかるのミステリー小説の映画化。
*阿部サダヲ（1970-）：日本の俳優。劇団大人計画所属。宮藤官九郎作品に多く出演し、映画『舞妓Haaaan!!!』（2007）で映画初主演。

*The Disease Called Capital Punishment：『死刑に至る病』（2022）。『悪人』の白石監督作品。櫛木理宇の同名小説を映画化したサイコサスペンス。

What is also most interesting is that the serial killer, played by Sadao Abe, only targeted high school students in school uniform. He sacrifices only such students, regardless of gender. This serial killer chose his victims based on age and school uniforms rather than gender. Should we say that he has a fetish for high school students, or a fetish for school uniforms? Whether it is desirable or not, it is progress if the public has come to recognize the **diversity** of human sexuality. In the prison scene with Kenshi Okada, their fingers touch each other, and you wonder if they are homosexual, but they are not. This ambiguity also reminds us of the complexity of human sexuality.

*fetish：フェチ。対象の身体的あるいは装飾的なパーツに対して性的魅力を感じる傾向・嗜好・趣味を指す言葉。

EXERCISE ③

次の各文が、リーディングの内容と一致していればTを、一致しなければFを選び、○をつけましょう。

	答え
① Incel is a community of men who become misogynists out of resentment at not being able to date women, and sometimes engage in violent attacks and accusations against women.	T ・ F
② Misogyny is not a term that has only appeared in the recent discussion of sexism.	T ・ F
③ People who live in a homosocial world don't just dislike homosexuality. They also abhor women as objects of sexual desire.	T ・ F
④ American films, which once portrayed women in a degrading way, have overcome this problem in recent years due to the feminist movement.	T ・ F
⑤ Those who participate in MGTOW are hoping to establish nonaggressive relationships with the women if possible.	T ・ F
⑥ Aversion to women was the main reason for turning a vulnerable young man, suffering from mental illness and caring for his mother in poverty, into a vicious villain, the Joker.	T ・ F
⑦ Even in Japan, where the concept of incel is not widespread, films such as *Birds without Names* and *Villains* are being produced, which focus on traumatized men.	T ・ F

EXERCISE ④ : Word Order

文構造と文の意味を意識しながら、次の [　　] 内の表現を並べ替えて、文法的にも意味的にも正しい文を作りましょう。

① All men who have difficulty building good relationships with women are not [with / as misanthropic, / agree / less / defined / much] incels.

② Although the incel identity is not recognized as a formal psychological condition, further research is needed to [for / inferior, victimized / who / feel / care / those], and lonely.

③ In the past, Disney films have clearly portrayed typical female and male figures, but recently they have taken [challenge / a new / break / stereotypes / to / on / down] of gender inequality.

④ Since the release of Joaquin Phoenix's new *Joker* film, it has been debated whether its idea is [white / violence / paean to / or a complex / incel / about] humanity.

⑤ The incel subculture takes a nihilistic approach to explaining why they are unattractive to women, based on the 'black pill' theory—that [women / is everything / and that men / lookism / inferior in / judged / by / to be] looks are excluded from the social power structure.

⑥ With a [view of / on / distorted / women / being trampled / by independent] in western societies, some incels seek refuge in Japanese women; that is to say, they easily grasp the false fantasy circulated in the media that Japanese women are submissive and easy to control.

⑦ Although the perceptions of male vulnerability are not yet accepted in Japan, [portray / emerging / attempting to / films / these issues / are].

EXERCISE ⑤：Discussion／Writing

次の問いかけに関して、自分の考えをまとめてみましょう。

① The number of young white men who agree with incels is on the rise, a recent study states. What changes do you think would occur in society if incel were to become popular in Japan?

② There is a general endorsement towards violence among incels. They consider collective violence to be instrumental and to serve four main purposes: to attract attention, to exact revenge, to reinforce masculinity and to bring about political change. Does this assertion of misogynist incels make males less vulnerable?

アメリカは多様性に富む社会ですが、歴史を通じて民族・人種にもとづく偏見や差別が存在してきました。とりわけ奴隷制に端を発する黒人差別は根強く、1950〜1960年代の公民権運動を経てもなお、白人と黒人間の溝は埋まっていません。他方日本には、アメリカのような人種差別はないように見えるかもしれませんが、実際はどうでしょうか。ここでは、アメリカの文化や社会と比較しながら、同調圧力の強い日本社会において、どのような問題が生じているのかを考えてみましょう。

PRE-EXERCISE

次の英語の映画タイトルから内容を推測しながら、語群の日本語タイトルと結びつけ、答えを書き入れましょう。

	答え		答え
① *Lee Daniels' the Butler* (2014)		④ *Selma* (2014)	
② *Free State of Jones* (2016)		⑤ *Gone with the Wind* (1939)	
③ *Guess Who's Coming to Dinner* (1967)		⑥ *Just Mercy* (2019)	

 語群

a. 『ニュートン・ナイト／自由の旗をかかげた男』　　b. 『風と共に去りぬ』

c. 『大統領の執事の涙』　　d. 『黒い司法 0%からの奇跡』

e. 『グローリー / 明日への行進』　　f. 『招かれざる客』

EXERCISE ①

次の文章はリーディング箇所で扱われている映画のあらすじです。文構造や文意を考えながら音声を聴いて、下線部に表現を書き入れてみましょう。

映画❶：『マイスモールランド』(*My Small Land*)

Sarya, a 17-year old Kurdish refugee girl, has been living in Japan with her family since she was a child. She goes to high school in Saitama, surrounded with good friends. She starts working part-time to (1)＿＿＿＿＿ money for college and meets Sota, a high school boy in Tokyo. One day, she learns that her family refugee status is (2)＿＿＿＿＿ , which (3)＿＿＿＿＿ her family from working and traveling across the city. Her father, who continues working for the family, is taken into custody for (4)＿＿＿＿＿ labor, when the situation for Sarya changes drastically.

映画❷：『グリーンブック』(*Green Book*)

Tony Lip, an Italian-American bouncer at a fancy New York nightclub, is hired (1)＿＿＿＿＿＿＿ as a driver and bodyguard by Dr. Shirley, a world-class African-American pianist. They go on an eight-week concert tour, traveling through the Deep South, with a "Green Book," a guidebook that lists local (2)＿＿＿＿＿ and facilities (3)＿＿＿＿＿ to black people. While (4)＿＿＿＿＿ racism and danger in a land where racial segregation still persists, the two men, completely different, develop an unexpected bond over the course of their journey.

EXERCISE ②

次の英語表現と最も意味の近い日本語表現を語群から選び、答えを書き入れてみましょう。

	答え		答え		答え
① when it comes to		⑥ criticize		⑪ immigrant	
② racial discrimination		⑦ wary of		⑫ fit in with	
③ feature		⑧ get ～ wrong		⑬ fortunate	
④ superior to		⑨ insensitive		⑭ endure	
⑤ complicated		⑩ tolerant		⑮ provide ～ with . . .	

 語群

a. 複雑な・込み入った　　　b. 寛容な・寛大な　　　c. 人種差別

d. ～に関していえば　　　e. ～を誤解・勘違いする　　f. ～を批判・非難する

g. 幸運な・運のよい　　　h. ～に鈍感な・気づかない　i. ～に…を与える

j. ～より上の・上位にある　k. ～に適合する・なじむ　　l. 移民

m. ～に耐える・～をがまんする　　n. ～に用心する・警戒して　o. 特徴・特質

READING

The United States has seen many severe incidents **when it comes to** Black issues. Even today, there are many movies that depict harsh **racial discrimination**, such as *12 Years a Slave*, but on the other hand, more and more movies depict friendship between whites and blacks, which seems to be a prominent **feature** of recent movies.

This probably started with *The Defiant Ones*, starring Sidney Poitier, but in the

*Black：黒人の、黒人種の（この意味ではしばしば大文字で始めて用いる）。

*シドニー・ポアチエ（1927-2022）。アメリカの俳優・映画監督。

1980s, a growing number of action movies began pairing black and white actors, such as *Lethal Weapon*, *48 Hrs.*, and *Men in Black*.

The most recent example of that is *Green Book*. This depicts the journey of an Italian-American driver and a black, gay musician. Since the musician is a celebrity by profession, he is socially **superior to** the chauffeur, even though he bears the double burden of being gay and black. The movie showed us how **complicated** discrimination is. Although movies portraying friendship between blacks and whites are sometimes **criticized** as hypocritical, such movies can be effective in bringing the races closer together.

*chauffeur：お抱え運転手

The United States is a melting pot of races. When I first went there, what terrified me more than anything else upon getting off the airplane was how many different kinds of people there were. Although there was nothing wrong, I experienced quite a culture shock when I saw the wide variety of hair color, skin color, and outfits. Moreover, no one was **wary of** me. In Japan, people would not normally ask a foreigner for directions; however, in the United States, people do not think of me as special, and so they do not mind asking me for directions.

On the other hand, an American teacher once told me that Americans even find it frightening that everyone is dressed the same and looks the same in Japan. Indeed, after many years of teaching at universities, I get the sense that every year there are students with a similar hair style, similar clothes, and similar facial features, all sitting in the same place taking classes. They look so much alike that I sometimes even **get** the students' names **wrong**.

Around the 1980s, it was said that the Japanese were professional racists. When I was studying in the United States, the then Prime Minister Yasuhiro Nakasone made a problematic remark, and some American people were offended, thinking "Japanese people don't realize that they are insulting the others." The Japanese are **insensitive to** racial discrimination because they live in a world of similarities.

*中曽根康弘元首相（1918-2019）。1986年9月におこなった講演で、アメリカの黒人やヒスパニック系の知的水準の低さに言及し、批判を浴びた。

Japan has changed considerably with the arrival of the 21st century. It seems that the number of foreigners living in Japan is increasing, and convenience stores are hiring many foreigners as part-timers. Are Japanese people gradually becoming **tolerant** of diversity?

Now, what about racial discrimination in Japan? Discrimination against non-

Japanese residents and against the Buraku communities are often taken up as problematic in Japan. A lot of movies, including *Pacchigi! Love and Peace*, *Blood & Bones*, *Go, and Yakiniku Dragon*, depict Korean people living in Japan, but their focus is on how those people live in Japan rather than on discrimination per se. These movies do not tackle the harsh discrimination against Koreans living in Japan, but rather portray them as a different culture within Japan.

One recent movie that I found very good is *My Small Land*. It is about a Kurdish **immigrant** girl who is losing her residency status in Japan, but her positive outlook on life leaves us feeling refreshed after watching the movie. This movie does not seem to focus on discrimination against foreigners, but rather it made me realize that Japan does not have adequate laws for accepting immigrants.

A serious problem in Japan, in contrast to the United States, may be that people strongly feel that they must be the same as others; they say "the nail that sticks out gets pounded down." Japan is a land of gut feeling and peer pressure, as described in *Physical Education: The Disease That Undermines Japan*, mentioned earlier.

In the United States, I find high school students there look much older. Even at 16, high school girls wear a lot of makeup, which can make them look like they are over 20 years old. The United States has a sexy culture, while Japan a cute culture. In the book, *Why Foreign Women Don't Wear Bangs*, Sandra Haefelin, suggests that Japanese women wear bangs probably because they want to look cute.

However, cute could also mean childish. Japanese children are kept under tight control until they reach high school graduate age, which leads to their uniformity. People who are different from the norm become the target of bullying. People with individuality, uniqueness, and self-assertiveness are not accepted. In Japan, there are no specific factors for discrimination and bullying such as skin color or religion as in the United States; but rather the inability to **fit in with** everyone else and thinking differently than others can become targets for discrimination and bullying.

Although education that values individuality has long been acknowledged in Japan, there are still many schools where baseball teams are forced to have a crew cut (which makes no sense). It can be said that Japanese people tend to

*Buraku communities：被差別部落。この地域に住む人たちへの差別を部落差別という。

*per se：それ自体で

*Kurdish：クルド人
*residency status：在留資格

*サンドラ・ヘフェリン著『体育会系　日本を蝕む病』(2020年)
※ Chapter 5 参照。

*『なぜ外国人女性は前髪を作らないのか』(2021年)。著者サンドラ・ヘフェリン (1975-) は、日本を活動拠点とするドイツ出身の作家、著述家。

*crew cut：角刈り。buzz cut ともいう。

feel closer to those who are the same as them.

This may be horrible for some students. Partly because of this situation, teachers are portrayed as evil in some recent Japanese movies, such as *Lesson of the Evil*, *Confessions*, and *Black School Rules*. At times, teachers are even portrayed as psychopaths. In Japan, where guts are valued, people tend to be persuaded that they must put up with the present situation by looking at others in harsher circumstances than themselves, thinking "because the world is full of people who are less **fortunate**" or "there was a time when people had to struggle to eat."

However, we have a problem with this idea. Everyone has a different idea of what they can and cannot **endure**. Also, as depicted in Frankl's masterpiece, *Man's Search for Meaning: An Introduction to Logotherapy*, human minds change according to the situation. As Maslow's hierarchy of needs shows, human needs go on to higher levels. It is true that for people kept in concentration camps for Jews, the athletic society of Japan may be nothing, but if that is the case, you have to be put in such a situation upon our birth. It will take more time to maintain homeostasis.

If we try to **provide** children living in the globalized and IT-oriented society **with** an education similar to that of the wartime period, it is certain that the number of children who suffer from mental illnesses will surely increase.

*Frankl's masterpiece：オーストリアの精神医学者ヴィクトール・E・フランクル（1905-1997）による、自身の体験にもとづくナチスの強制収容所の記録（1947年。1977年に新版刊行）。邦題は『夜と霧』。

*Maslow：アブラハム・マズロー（1908-1970）。アメリカの心理学者。著書『人間性の心理学』（1954年）において、人間の欲求は階層から成るとする欲求階層説を提唱した。

*concentration camp：強制収容所

*homeostasis：ホメオスタシス、動的平衡、恒常性

EXERCISE ③ --

次の各文が、リーディングの内容と一致していれば T を、一致しなければ F を選び、○をつけましょう。

	答え
① Only a few American movies have depicted an interracial friendship so far.	T・F
② In the movie *Green Book*, an Italian-American chauffer suffers terrible double discrimination.	T・F
③ The writer was struck by the diversity of people at the airport on his first trip to the United States.	T・F
④ According to the writer, we find more foreigners living and working in Japan in recent years.	T・F
⑤ According to the writer, some Japanese movies, portraying Korean people in Japan, focus on serious racial discrimination.	T・F

	答え
⑥ Referring to Sandra Haefelin's book, the writer argues that American women value cuteness rather than sexiness.	T・F
⑦ The writer suggests that being different from others might cause discrimination and bullying in Japan.	T・F

EXERCISE ④ ： Word Order --

文構造と文の意味を意識しながら、次の〔　　〕内の表現を並べ替えて、文法的にも意味的にも正しい文を作りましょう。

① Discrimination is the〔act / down / of / people / put others / who〕for certain characteristics.

② Some English speakers would〔boys / associate / Japanese / wear / the uniforms / high school〕with a military style.

③ The Kurdish people have been persecuted in Turkey as an ethnic minority without a country, and some〔as / fled to / have / of them / refugees to / Japan〕escape such persecution.

④ It is important〔a childhood / that bullying / not just / to / remember / is〕problem.

⑤ According to a survey, 76 percent of women in America〔at / bangs / have had / in / life / some point / their〕.

⑥ The common belief that the Japanese are collectivist was first popularized by the American anthropologist Ruth Benedict's book, *The Chrysanthemum and the Sword*,〔after / published / shortly / which / the end / was〕of World War II.

⑦ What makes Frankl's book appealing to people throughout the ages is that it is not merely an indictment of concentration camps, [all about / life / a questioning / is / but rather / of / what].

EXERCISE ⑤ : Discussion／Writing

次の問いかけに関して、自分の考えをまとめてみましょう。

① Some people argue that school uniforms should be banned because they prevent students from freely expressing themselves and exploring their individuality. What is your opinion on this issue and explain why.

② What are some examples of racial（or any other kind of）discrimination that you have seen or heard about in your neighborhood, school, or job?

Chapter 12 Romance

この 50 年間の社会の変化や技術革新を経て、若者の恋愛観もまた大きく変化を遂げています。結婚に対する意識が変化し、恋愛や結婚に縛られない考え方が普通になりつつあります。また、男女の役割への期待が変化し、性別役割に固執しないパートナーシップという価値観が広がりました。セクシュアリティの多様性も認知されるようになり、パートナーシップの選択肢自体が多様化しているといえます。日本やアメリカの映画において、そうした変化がいかに反映されているかを考えながら、読み進めていきましょう。

PRE-EXERCISE

次の英語の映画タイトルから内容を推測しながら、語群の日本語タイトルと結びつけ、答えを書き入れましょう。

	答え		答え
① *Something's Gotta Give* (2003)		④ *Eternal Sunshine of the Spotless Mind* (2004)	
② *Beach Rats* (2017)		⑤ *Wonder Wheel* (2017)	
③ *Rachel Getting Married* (2008)		⑥ *The Time Traveler's Wife* (2009)	

 語群

a. 『男と女の観覧車』 b. 『恋愛適齢期』

c. 『レイチェルの結婚』 d. 『ブルックリンの片隅で』

e. 『きみがぼくを見つけた日』 f. 『エターナル・サンシャイン』

EXERCISE ①

次の文章はリーディング箇所で扱われている映画のあらすじです。文構造や文意を考えながら音声を聴いて、下線部に表現を書き入れてみましょう。

映画❶：『ちょっと思い出しただけ』(*Just Remembering*)

The man used to be a dancer, but since his leg injury, he works as a lighting engineer. The woman is a (1)_____ driver. This is a rather quirky, yet (2)_____ love story that (3)_____ the six years between the "end" and the "beginning" of a relationship between a man and a woman, year by year. Finally, the meaning of the title *Just Remembering* will (4)_____ deeply into your heart.

映画❷：『キャロル』(*Carol*)

During the Christmas season in New York City, Therese, working in a department store in Manhattan, is (1)＿＿＿＿＿＿ Carol, an elegant woman who is looking for a gift for her daughter. Carol is in divorce (2)＿＿＿＿＿＿ with her husband and is fighting for (3)＿＿＿＿＿＿ of their daughter. The film depicts love among two women and the deep bond that (4)＿＿＿＿＿＿ in them.

EXERCISE ②

次の英語表現と最も意味の近い日本語表現を語群から選び、答えを書き入れてみましょう。

	答え		答え		答え
① publish		⑥ lofty		⑪ dissolution	
② eccentric		⑦ elopement		⑫ obsess	
③ bachelor		⑧ mutual		⑬ racial	
④ make ends meet		⑨ reminisce		⑭ obstacle	
⑤ powerhouse		⑩ creature		⑮ phenomenon	

語群

a. 追憶する　　　　b. 相互の　　　　　c. 収支を合わせる
d. 解消　　　　　　e. 出版する　　　　f. 人種（上）の
g. 生き物　　　　　h. 非常に高い　　　i. 現象
j. 風変わりな　　　k. 独身男性　　　　l. 障害（物）
m. （妄想などが）取りつく　n. 強力な組織　　o. 駆け落ち

READING

These days, the issue of singleness has become a social problem in Japan. A book titled *Young People Who Don't Fall in Love: Convenience Store Sex and Cost-effective Marriage* has even been **published**. Up to the 20th century, most people were married, and only about 3% of both men and women were unmarried. Those who were single at 40 were considered **eccentric**. Today, one in four men is, however, a lifelong **bachelor**, and 15% of women also end their lives without ever being married.

Until about the 1980s, many college-aged women said that falling in love means getting married as it was commonly believed that a woman would not

*Young People who Don't Fall in Love: Convenience Store Sex and Cost-effective Marriage (『恋愛しない若者たち　コンビニ化する性とコスパ化する結婚』)：牛窪恵による、2015年に出版された本。

find a job after graduating from a four-year college. At that time, people said that a woman's life was like Christmas cake, meaning that she could be sold if she was up to the age of 23 or 24, but if she was past 25, she was old stock. Since men were still employed for life in those days and usually worked for the same company for a long time, companies did not want to hire a 22-year-old woman with a college degree because they knew that she would only work for about a year anyway even if they hired her. For women, employment was more likely for junior college and high school graduates.

Men, as well, until around the 1980s, had a sense that it was cooler to be a man who did not "let the women do the work." Many male students wanted to have the I'm-feeding-my-family feeling - and therefore wanted their wives to stay in the house after marriage.

The bubble economy then burst, however, plunging the country into a recession and skyrocketing tuition fees. Today, women must also work to **make ends meet** for most families. If women did not work, they would not be able to get married. To be a full-time housewife has become a **lofty** goal.

And now comes the I-may-not-marry syndrome. When I asked people who say 'I may not marry' why, financial problems were the main reason for not marrying. When single, women can spend all the money they earn, but this is not the case when they get married. As a single person, one can eat, sleep, and take a bath whenever, married people do not have that freedom. Furthermore, many young students nowadays might think, "I'm not sure I can love one person for decades." In the 100-year lifespan era, life is too long to stay with the person you loved when you were young.

When it comes to love, youngsters today are cool. Whereas in the old days, there would have been romantic relationships where love was all that mattered, with suicide, **elopement**, wrist cutting, and **mutual** dependence, today's young people would not do such things, because it would be considered ridiculous. That's what I feel when I watch recent movies.

In *Just Remembering*, we find a love story in which the couple does not step into the other person's shoes when possible. The story focuses on young people who are too self-protective and hesitant to put energy into love. The last scene in the film shows the heroine, now married, **reminiscing** about an old boyfriend, and the man she is married to holding and taking care of her

*バブル経済の崩壊：
1980年代後半の泡
（バブル）のような
急速な好景気を経
て、1991年〜1993
年に起こった景気後
退期（株価や地価の
急速な暴落）を指す。
*I-may-not-marry
syndrome（結婚し
ないかもしれない症
候群）：バブル時代
に出版された谷村志
穂著のノンフィク
ション『結婚しない
かもしれない症候
群』（1990年）は、
婚期を過ぎて一人で
生きる女性の恋愛・
結婚観を取材し、働
く女性たちの圧倒的
な支持を得た。

child. It is the time of *ikumen* (men who care for their children).

In *I fell in love like a flower bouquet*, two people before their relationship become lovers' one sleep together but do not have sex. Later, they become lovers, continue to live together, and then dissolve their relationship, but they continue to live together for a while after the **dissolution**. It further depicts that even if they both have new lovers after the breakup, they do not hate the other for this.

Perhaps in many cases, young people today fall in love with someone they like in their own way, break up when things don't work out, and then go out with someone new. It's not like the old days' romance, which was only with one person. They are not **obsessed** with making love. So even if they break up, they don't hate each other, and can restart as friends.

The main character in *The Real Thing* is a man who, for some reason, refuses to break off an unsavory relationship with a woman with whom he has not had sex and who keeps annoying him. "There are people like me, too," the man says. "Not all of them live their lives following their desires." Nowadays, love affairs and having sex are not as important as they used to be.

What is the situation in the U.S.? These days, male-female romance in the U.S. is depicted mostly in romantic comedies and less frequently in drama films. After all, considering that there was plenty of melodrama in the Douglas Sirk era of the 1950s, romance is becoming less common in the United States, as well.

The standard pattern of love stories, such as *The Notebook* and *Loving*, is that love is fueled by obstacles, such as different social status or **racial** differences. However, now that status and racial differences are no longer as much of an **obstacle** to love as they used to be, a growing trend in film settings is the romance between same-sex couples. With romantic films like *Carol* and *Call Me By Your Name*, one might say that homosexuality is the most common form of love.

It is likely that heterosexuality is no longer amusing enough to be made into a drama. We may be in an era of the decline of heterosexuality. Heterosexuality began to be popular about 50 years ago, and it was only in the 1970s that love marriages began to surpass arranged marriages in Japan.

*イクメン：育児をする男性の略語。厚生労働省の「イクメンプロジェクト」においては、イクメンとは、「子育てを楽しみ、自分自身も成長する男性のこと」とある。

*romantic comedy（ロマンティック・コメディ）：映画のジャンルの一つ。恋愛をテーマにしたコメディのこと。
*drama film（ドラマ映画）：映画のジャンルの一つ。主として、シリアス寄りのドラマティックな人間模様を描いた、いわゆるヒューマン・ドラマを指すことが多い。

*heterosexuality：異性愛

*arranged marriage：お見合い結婚

The U.S. is a divorce **powerhouse**, with half of marriages ending in divorce. Likewise, one-third of the married population in Japan also gets divorced. We have no dreams about marriage and feel indifferent to it if it goes on like this.

In the United States, these days, there are some movies portraying romances with something other than human beings. *The Shape of Water* is a love story between a mute woman and a male underwater **creature**. *Her* is about a man who falls in love with an automated phone voice.

This **phenomenon** reminds us that the age of minorities and diversity has arrived. The "no love between men and women" syndrome might be occurring in the United States.

*離婚率：日本において「3組に1組が離婚している」というのは、（婚姻したカップルのうち、何組が離婚したか、ということではなく）単純に同じ年の婚姻件数と離婚件数を比較した場合の率を指すに過ぎない。

EXERCISE ③

次の各文が、リーディングの内容と一致していればTを、一致しなければFを選び、〇をつけましょう。

	答え
① Women in Japan were more likely to find work as junior college graduates than as four-year college graduates until the 1980s.	T・F
② Due to the recession that followed the bursting of the bubble economy, women aspired to be engaged in their employment rather than as a full-time housewife.	T・F
③ Many recent films have portrayed young characters obsessed with seeking romance. They believe love is everything.	T・F
④ According to the writer, today's young people do not care about being in love with one person. They easily end their relationships and continue a friend-like relationship after a breakup.	T・F
⑤ In the 1950s, romance was not as well-represented in American films as it is today.	T・F
⑥ The author says that recent films have shown that differences in social status and race are unlikely to be an obstacle.	T・F
⑦ Along with the decline of heterosexuality, in both the U.S. and Japan, a large majority of the population is divorced.	T・F

EXERCISE ④ : Word Order

文構造と文の意味を意識しながら、次の [   ] 内の表現を並べ替えて、文法的にも意味的にも正しい文を作りましょう。

① In the past, a woman's age was compared to a Christmas cake. Namely, the expression ridiculed the age of 25 as the proper age for women to get married, [the cake / a / at / fixed / given / that / sold / is] price on the 25th, the day of Christmas.

② In the late 1990s, after the bursting of the bubble in the Japanese economy, [that / of / of / exceeded / the number / households / "dual income"] households with full-time housewives.

③ The term "the 100-year life" was coined and popularized by London Business School professors in their book. The United Nations estimates that the number of people in Japan over [age / one / more / 100 years / of / than / will / surpass] million by 2050.

④ The *Ikumen* Project, launched by the Ministry of Health, Labor and Welfare in 2010, intends to increase social momentum [to / to / a / more / men / encourage / take / working] active role in childcare and to take childcare leave.

⑤ Douglas Sirk was a German filmmaker best known for his Hollywood melodramas of the 1950s. Many [a / his films / commercial / of / success / huge / were], but they were fiercely reviewed by critics at the outset.

⑥ When we say that "one in three couples divorce" in Japan, it is simply [comparing / the result / the number / marriages / of / of] and divorces in the same year, and it does not indicate the actual percentage of divorced couples.

⑦ In a social trend toward a greater respect for diversity, a certain number [view / and marriage / of / as / love / young people] merely one of a variety of options in life although it would be premature to conclude that young people are moving away from romance.

EXERCISE ⑤ : Discussion／Writing

> 次の問いかけに関して、自分の考えをまとめてみましょう。

① Nowadays, the issue of love can be viewed as related to social problems, such as unmarried people, late marriages, and declining birthrates as a result of young people's growing trend away from romance. Is romance a social problem that can be linked to marriage and family? State your opinion on this issue.

② Among the measures that the Japanese government has put forth as part of its "100-year life plan" is the role of a romantic relationship. How is romance necessary for you to live a prosperous and peaceful 100-year life? Please explain your thoughts along with your reasons.

日本は、2007年に超高齢社会へと突入しました。高齢者（65歳以上）率が21%以上を占め、今後もこの高齢者率は高くなり、2060年には約40%に達すると予測されています。また、海外の動向としても、日本同様、特に先進諸国で少子高齢化が進行中です。日本でかつては珍しかった百歳以上の高齢者は、2022年には90,526人と増加傾向にあります。人生100年時代と言われるこれからの時代、私たちは老年期をどのように過ごすべきなのでしょうか。本章では、高齢者をジェンダーの視点で考察し、国際比較を通して、老年期の在り方について考えてみましょう。

PRE-EXERCISE

次の英語の映画タイトルから内容を推測しながら、語群の日本語タイトルと結びつけ、答えを書き入れましょう。

	答え		答え
① *Up*（2009）		④ *5 Flights Up*（2014）	
② *The First Grader*（2010）		⑤ *Secondhand Lions*（2003）	
③ *Remember*（2015）		⑥ *Book Club*（2018）	

語群

a. 『手紙は憶えている』　　　　b. 『ウォルター少年と、夏の休日』
c. 『また、あなたとブッククラブで』　　d. 『カールじいさんの空飛ぶ家』
e. 『おじいさんと草原の小学校』　　f. 『ニューヨーク　眺めのいい部屋売ります』

EXERCISE ①

次の文章はリーディング箇所で扱われている映画のあらすじです。文構造や文意を考えながら音声を聴いて、下線部に表現を書き入れてみましょう。

映画❶：『キネマの神様』（*God of Cinema*）

Go once aspired to be a film director, but his dream was
（1）＿＿＿＿＿＿. In his later years, his wife and daughter
（2）＿＿＿＿＿＿ him due to his gambling debts. His grandson,
Yuta, was so（3）＿＿＿＿＿＿ with the script of Go's first film that
he suggested that Go enter a screenwriting contest. As a result, Go
（4）＿＿＿＿＿＿ his love for film.

映画❷：『最高の人生の見つけ方』(*The Bucket List*)

> Carter, a kindhearted mechanic, and Edward, an (1)＿＿＿＿＿＿＿＿
> businessman, (2)＿＿＿＿＿＿ together in the hospital. Having been
> told they have only six (3)＿＿＿＿＿＿ to live, they hit it off and
> (4)＿＿＿＿＿＿ on a journey to do all the things they want to do in
> life, with a bucket list, which is a list of things they want to do before
> they die.

ＥXERCISE ② --

次の英語表現と最も意味の近い日本語表現を語群から選び、答えを書き入れてみましょう。

	答え		答え		答え
① depiction		⑥ contemplate		⑪ henchman	
② unworthy		⑦ ultimately		⑫ rampage	
③ care for		⑧ childcare leave		⑬ revel in	
④ solemnly		⑨ distress		⑭ face off against	
⑤ lovingly		⑩ unscrupulous		⑮ indulge in	

語群

a. 愛情に満ちて	b. 困窮	c. ～をじっくり考える
d. まじめに	e. 育児休暇	f. 暴れ回ること
g. 不実な	h. （空想など）にふける	i. 描写
j. 結局	k. ～を心配する	l. 賞賛に値しない
m. 子分	n. ～と対決する	o. ～に夢中になる

ＲEADING --

God of Cinema is indeed a well-made film directed by master filmmaker Yoji Yamada. The film was originally intended for Ken Shimura to play the lead role, but he died of COVID-19, so Kenji Sawada was chosen to fill in for him. Director Yoji Yamada is almost 90 years old. The actors who played the main roles in his films, such as Kiyoshi Atsumi, Ken Takakura, and Rentaro Mikuni, have all passed away. I wonder what it feels like to be the only one alive among them, and to be still active as a director. Come to think of it, his wife passed away a long time ago, too.

The movie is about an old man who cannot give up his love for the movie

*山田洋次（1931-）：日本の映画監督、脚本家、演出家。『男はつらいよ』シリーズなど人情劇を発表し、現役でキネマ旬報ベストテンに最多入賞。日本映画界の第一人者。

business, played by Kenji Sawada, and Masaki Suda plays the character as a youth. What interested me more than anything else was Kenji Sawada's selfish, no-good attitude. He is almost 80 years old and still a child. His wife and daughter are there to support him. Director Yamada is best known for his Tora-san series, which many feminist women have criticized because of his **depiction** of a woman who accepts a selfish, spoiled man. Tora-san's younger sister, Sakura-san, is angered by Torajiro, the **unworthy** older brother, but still **cares for** him.

*no-good：（人が）
役に立たない

*feminist：男女同権
主義者

When I was in graduate school, I read a book in a class titled *Bread Givers*, a novel by a Jewish woman writer, Anzia Yezierska. In this novel, the father is a Jewish rabbi. In the case of Jewish rabbis, it seems that women are expected to do all the work and housework, and men are allowed to **solemnly revel in** their faith. This is exactly the same as the father played by Kenji Sawada. However, in *Bread Givers*, the main character, the youngest daughter, looks at her father and her mother and sisters who live according to his customs with a critical eye, and the theme of the film is her conflict. However, the women in *God of Cinema* seem to affirm their spoiled father entirely because they accept him even though they complain about him. The film **lovingly** embraces the man who can only live this way.

*アンジア・イージアス
カ（1880-1970）：
ユダヤ系アメリカ人
小説家。
*rabbi：ラビ（ユダ
ヤ教の指導者）

It is truly the world of Yoji Yamada, but many of his fans are women. Perhaps it resonates with the mentality of the Japanese people. As Hayao Kawai says, Japan is a maternal society. In *A Long Goodbye*, in which Tsutomu Yamazaki plays the father, the focus is on the wife and daughters taking care of the aging father.

*河合隼雄（1928-
2007）：心理学者。
専門は分析心理学
（ユング心理学）、臨
床心理学、日本文
化。
*maternal：母性の
⇔ paternal 父性の

Only the Cat Knows depicts the retirement of a married couple. In this film, the wife, who has been dissatisfied with her life with her husband, with whom she never speaks, although they have a peaceful home, is **contemplating** divorce. Then Chibi, the cat, disappears. The mother decides to hire a pet detective to try to find Chibi. In this film, too, we see the interaction between a husband whose interests lie outside the family and a wife who is annoyed by her husband but **ultimately** cannot stay away from him. Young men today may not go this far, but many of these men are from the generation that spent their younger days during the period of high economic growth, working dedicatedly only for a living and never taking paid or **childcare leave**.

*the period of high
economic growth：
高度経済成長期。
1955 年〜 1973 年の
19 年間を指す。戦
後の焼け野原の何も
ない場所から熾烈な
勢いの電撃的制覇に
より基盤を築いた時
期。
*paid leave：有給休
暇

In American movies, you rarely see wives complaining about their husbands.

If that were the case in Europe or the U.S., they would probably leave each other. In Japan, however, people complain about each other but continue to stay married without leaving each other.

Like in Japan, men in the U.S. are depicted as childlike for their age. "Age well and stay energetic! Be macho!" This is, however, men's mindset in the U.S. The so-called "anti-aging" mentality is deeply rooted among men.

In *The Bucket List*, the bucket list in the title is a list of things you want to do before you die, and the story is about old men who have been told they have only six months left to live and are bouncing around trying to do the things they want to do before they die. Similarly, *Grudge Match* is a story about old people boxing. Sylvester Stallone played a boxer in his younger days in *Rocky* and Robert De Niro in *Raging Bull*, but this time they play boxers in a comedy. "We can still fight!" That is what is depicted in this film.

In *Dirty Grandpa*, De Niro plays an old man who travels around in a car with Zac Efron, performs on stage naked to the waist, and finally marries and has children with a much younger woman. In *The Intern*, he plays an old man who has retired, whose wife has died, and who volunteers to be an intern at the age of 70. He now seems to specialize in playing old men who try to stay young despite their age. *Going in Style* is another comedy about an all-male group of bad old men. De Niro also starred in a film in the same vein called *Last Vegas*. The U.S. has always had a long history of depicting boyish old men, such as in *Cocoon*, a film about a retirement home.

Even in Japanese cinema, Takeshi Kitano's *Ryuzo and His Seven Henchmen* tells the story of a group of retired old yakuza who **face off against** a group of young men who are doing whatever they want with "It's me" scams, which are phone scams involving calls from pretended relatives in **distress**, and **unscrupulous** door-to-door selling. The poster visuals also include Ryuzo and his seven **henchmen** along with the words, "Old men are the best!! We don't need tomorrow!!," and the story is about the **rampage** of eight unique old men. However, this **rampage** is more of an influence from American films.

In general, Japanese old men are childish in that they are forever dependent on women. American old men are childish in that they want to do the same things as young boys with other men forever. Do men remain children until the end of their lives?

*macho：（筋肉・体型などで）男らしさをひけらかす
語源はスペイン語。
*bucket list：バケツリスト
死ぬ前にやっておきたいことや達成したいことを書き出したリスト。

*retirement home：老人ホーム

*"It's me" scams：オレオレ詐欺

*door-to-door selling：訪問販売

Moreover, these films depict these men in a positive light. Of course, this is because it is a male-directed film, and if it had been made by a female director, the story might not be like this, but perhaps the desire not to lose one's childlike spirit all the time is a psychology shared by men in both Japan and the United States.

*male-directed： 男性監督による direct（～を監督する）。

Of course, in reality there are many more miserable old men, but since it is a movie, I guess the viewers are just going to **indulge in** fantasy for a while. It is a fantasy that will cheer up old men.

*cheer up：～を元気づける

EXERCISE ③ ---

次の各文が、リーディングの内容と一致していればＴを、一致しなければＦを選び、〇をつけましょう。

	答え
① The film *God of Cinema* was intended for Kenji Sawada to play the lead role from the beginning.	T・F
② Many feminist women have been critical of the Tora-san series because Director Yamada depicted a woman accepting a selfish, spoiled man.	T・F
③ The novel *Bread Givers* depicts the youngest daughter critically looking at her father who is a Jewish rabbi.	T・F
④ The women in the film *God of Cinema* seemingly deny their spoiled father completely without accepting him.	T・F
⑤ The writer argues that the "anti-aging" mentality is deep-rooted among men in the United States.	T・F
⑥ American films have long depicted boyish old guys, such as in *Cocoon*, a film about a retirement home.	T・F
⑦ According to the writer, Japanese old men are childish in that they are eternally independent from women.	T・F

文構造と文の意味を意識しながら、次の〔　〕内の表現を並べ替えて、文法的にも意味的にも正しい文を作りましょう。

---

① A rabbi is a Jewish religious leader 〔 studies / academic / qualified after / completing / is / who 〕 of Jewish history and texts.

---

② Hayao Kawai was a Japanese Jungian 〔 therapy to / psychologist / Japanese psychology / introduced sandplay / who 〕.

---

③ It is important to ensure 〔 treated / elderly in / that / our society / the / are 〕 with the respect and dignity they deserve.

---

④ The number of people aged 65 and over in the United 〔 since / States / has / growth / increased steadily / with accelerated 〕 2011.

---

⑤ Many studies show that social interaction, such as strong, happy relationships with family 〔 closely related / is / friends, / to good / and / health and 〕 longevity.

---

⑥ The elderly need to beware of cash card collection 〔 visit / which / homes / scams in / swindlers / their 〕 to trick them into handing over their cards.

---

⑦ Most research supports that staying busy, maintaining social 〔 meaning in our / daily routine are / connections, / connected to / and finding 〕 healthy aging.

EXERCISE ⑤ : Discussion／Writing

次の問いかけに関して、自分の考えをまとめてみましょう。

① The media affects how people view the elderly in our society. How are older men and women portrayed in advertisements in your culture? Do you find any gender differences in how they are portrayed in advertisements? If yes, explain how they are different.

② If you were a film director, how would you depict the elderly in your film? Why?

Chapter 14 LGBT

アメリカでは、同性婚やトランスジェンダーをはじめとする LGBT 問題は論争の的であり続けています。政治情勢にも影響されるため、LGBT の権利を巡る状況は一進一退の様相です。日本でも遅ればせながら、LGBT 関連の案件が議論の俎上に載せられることが増えており、このこと自体は好ましい前進でしょう。しかし、抜本的な状況改善にはまだまだ程遠いのが現実です。LGBT 問題の劇的な進展を妨げる一要因は、同性愛嫌悪の傾向が強い（強硬な）保守層の反発でしょう。LGBT の権利を否定的に語る人たちが挙げる理由にはどのようなものがあるのか、またそれは正当なものなのか、ということを考えながら、本章の内容を検討しましょう。

PRE-EXERCISE

次の英語の映画タイトルから内容を推測しながら、語群の日本語タイトルと結びつけ、答えを書き入れましょう。

	答え		答え
① *Boys Erased*（2018）		④ *The Hours*（2002）	
② *The Danish Girl*（2015）		⑤ *Ammonite*（2020）	
③ *Pride*（2014）		⑥ *Beginners*（2010）	

語群

a.『アンモナイトの目覚め』　　b.『パレードへようこそ』

c.『ある少年の告白』　　d.『人生はビギナーズ』

e.『リリーのすべて』　　f.『めぐりあう時間たち』

EXERCISE ①

次の文章はリーディング箇所で扱われている映画のあらすじです。文構造や文意を考えながら音声を聴いて、下線部に表現を書き入れてみましょう。

映画❶：『ミッドナイトスワン』（*Midnight Swan*）

Nagisa lives in Tokyo as a transgender woman, while (1)＿＿＿＿＿＿ her gender identity from her relatives back home in Hiroshima. Nagisa is asked to (2)＿＿＿＿＿ her relative's daughter Ichika, who is an (3)＿＿＿＿＿ teenager. In Tokyo, a ballet teacher notices Ichika's talent in ballet. At first Nagisa thinks Ichika is an obstacle, but gradually begins to feel affection, similar to (4)＿＿＿＿＿ of a mother, and wants to contribute to Ichika's dream.

映画❷：『カサブランカ』（*Casablanca*）

> In 1941, Casablanca, a city in the French territory of Morocco, is
> (1) _____ under the (2) _____ of Nazi Germany.
> Many people are trying to flee into exile to escape the looming Nazi
> crisis. Rick, an American, sees Ilsa, who was his lover in Paris before
> the fall, at the bar he runs. Ilsa's husband Laszlo is a leader of the
> (3) _____ movement (4) _____ by Nazi Germany. Ilsa
> and Laszlo are trying to escape Casablanca.

EXERCISE ②

次の英語表現と最も意味の近い日本語表現を語群から選び、答えを書き入れてみましょう。

	答え		答え		答え
① approve of		⑥ prominent		⑪ latently	
② pass		⑦ go to such lengths		⑫ lament	
③ make the headlines		⑧ adaptation		⑬ immortal	
④ repression		⑨ replete with		⑭ inclination	
⑤ prevalent		⑩ abbreviation		⑮ eliminate	

語群

a. そこまでする	b. 溢れて・満ちて	c. 短縮・略語
d. 潜在的に	e. 賛成する・認める	f. 不朽の・不滅の
g. 嘆き悲しむ	h. 抑圧	i. 新聞の見出しに載る
j. 広く行き渡っている	k. なくす・除去する	l. 翻案・脚色
m. 顕著な・目立つ	n. 可決する・承認する	o. 傾向・性向

READING

Many people seem to think that the LGBT situation is even more difficult in Japan than in the United States. This may be partly because Japan does not **approve of** same-sex marriage, even though all of the other G7 countries do. On the other hand, however, hate crimes often occur in the United States, and some people are even murdered simply because they are LGBT. For this reason, the Matthew Shepard Act was **pass**ed to prevent hate crimes.

In Japan, we rarely hear about LGBT people being killed. Recently, the debate on whether or not to allow same-sex marriage has been **making the headlines**

*LGBT：Lesbian, Gay, Bisexual, Transgender
*same-sex marriage：同性婚。日本を除く G7 諸国では認められている。アジアでは台湾が 2019 年 5 月に法認。
*hate crimes：人種、民族、性指向などを理由とする偏見などに基づく犯罪。

in the Japanese media, but it is generally believed that Japan has a lower level of oppression against LGBT people than Europe or the United States. It takes a lot of effort and financial resources to change society and laws. Since **repression** is less **prominent** in Japan than in the West, people in Japan may not be willing to **go to such lengths** to change the society.

In Japan, as in the United States, homosexuality has long been depicted in novels and movies. Soseki Natsume's *Kokoro*, one of the most celebrated works of Japanese literature, is regarded as a homosexual novel. The film **adaptation** of *Kokoro*, directed by Kon Ichikawa, depicts the relationships among three handsome actors, Masayuki Mori, Tatsuya Mihashi, and Shoji Yasui, all with beautiful romanticism, and would have been labeled as a homosexual film today.

Shintaro Ishihara was also a politician and writer who was well known for his homophobic views against gays, but ironically, films based on his novels portray a world that is very "gayish." Films such as *Season of Violence* and *Crazed Fruit*, starring Shintaro's younger brother, Yujiro Ishihara, depict the youth of that era, known as the "Taiyou Zoku" or "Sun Gang." The scenes of men playing naked at the beach are well portrayed, making us feel as if we were watching a so-called gay film.

Kimio Ito calls this kind of gay-like male-male relationship "homoeroticism." Even in American films, dramas featuring male friendships, such as *Top Gun* and *Fight Club*, are **replete with** scenes featuring naked men. In Ito's view, homoeroticism refers to a passionate connection between men who do not sexually cross the line, but are willing to sacrifice their lives together in a war.

It can also be argued that all men are inherently and **latently** homosexual. In fact, as indicated in Shoji Momoyama's book *Why Men Tend to Prefer Male Friends to Lovers*, men tend to prefer movies portraying male-male friendships to those portraying romantic relationships with women. This tendency is particularly strong in America, and even in the 21st century, it is frequently **lamented** that Hollywood is still male-oriented, with few actresses in the cast. American films have long been said to have homosexual undertones, but this is due to the fact that many of them are male-male dramas.

For example, the very last scene of the **immortal** masterpiece *Casablanca* is all too well known. Rick the protagonist, who has broken up with his girlfriend

*夏目漱石（1867-1916）：代表作は『吾輩は猫である』、『坊っちゃん』など。千円札に肖像画が使われたこともある。

*homophobic：同性愛嫌悪の。名詞形はhomophobiaである。
*-ish：〜っぽい、〜くらい、〜頃という意を示す表現。
*石原裕次郎（1934-1987）：昭和を代表する俳優の一人。

*桃山商事：恋バナ収集ユニット。著書やウェブ・雑誌・新聞連載、メディア出演など多数。

*male-oriented：男性優位の。
-oriented で〜志向の、〜を重視するの意。
*protagonist：主人公、主役。それに対して antagonist は敵対者、競争相手。

Ilsa, says, "Louis, I think this is the beginning of a beautiful friendship." Then he walks into the fog, together with Captain Louis Renault.

Men are more likely than women to discriminate against homosexuals, and it can be said that this is nothing more than a desire to deny their homosexual **inclination** as a part of themselves. Due to this, men tend to reject any tendency toward homosexuality in themselves.

*nothing more than：
〜に過ぎない、〜で
しかない。

In the 21st century, however, as the LGBT presence has become more **prevalent**, movies about male friendships seem to have gradually become more akin to gay movies, and "bromance" and BL movies have become more prominent. The term "bromance" is an **abbreviation** of "brother & romance" and refers to a buddy relationship between men who are as close as brothers. *Ted* and *The Hangover* are typical examples of such movies.

*BL：和 製 英 語 の
"Boys Love" を略し
た表現。男 性 同 士
の恋愛などを題材
とする小説や漫画
のジャンル。"Boys'
Love" と表記する場
合もある。

In Japan, there may not be many movies befitting the term "bromance," but there are many scenes of men bathing together, such as the scene in *Under the Open Sky*, where Koji Yakusho and Taiga Nakano enjoy a hot spring bath together. Thus, the Japanese hot spring culture may be considered a kind of Japanese "bromance" culture.

Japan is considered to be the birthplace of the BL culture.   Although the number of male fans of BL stories has recently been increasing, this culture basically originated from female fans called "fujoshi." They find male-female romance stories boring, because they see them only in relation to their femininity. They love BL stories so as to objectively enjoy the drama.

*腐女子；Boys Love
などの男性同性愛を
扱った漫画などの作
品や二次創作作品を
好む女性と指す表
現。これらを好む男
性は腐男子と呼ばれ
る。

Recent Japanese films featuring gay characters include *Close-Knit*, *Midnight Swan*, *The Cornered Mouse Dreams of Cheese*, *Rage*, and *Three Stories of Love*. In these films, good-looking actors, who are popular among female fans, have taken on gay roles. In the United States, there are also gay films that beautifully depict love between handsome men, such as *My Own Private Idaho*, *Brokeback Mountain*, and *Call Me by Your Name*, but the trend seems to be more prevalent in Japan. This is probably because "fujoshi" girls enjoy watching beautiful men and the dramas. This kind of situation seems to be effective in **eliminating** prejudice against LGBT people.

One of the most innovative Japanese gay films/dramas is *Ossan's Love*. The word gay is almost never mentioned in this work. The main characters, Soichi Haruta（Kei Tanaka）and Musashi（Kotaro Yoshida）, are both ordinary businessmen who also socialize with women. They are not aware of their own gayness.

*gayness：ゲイであること。同性の人に性的に惹かれること。

The problem, though, is that the film is a comedy. In Japan, gay entertainers like Matsuko Deluxe and others have always had a tendency to make themselves the subject of laughter. Nevertheless, for the people concerned, gay discrimination is still a very serious issue, and there was even a news about a young man who committed suicide due to being outed.

Although people may not be murdered for being LGBT as the United States, it is still a problem in Japan that people make it into a self-deprecating joke. The time has come to think about LGBT issues more earnestly, and in fact, universities are nowadays giving more consideration to LGBT students.

*self-deprecating：自嘲的な、自虐的な。

EXERCISE ③ --

次の各文が、リーディングの内容と一致していれば T を、一致しなければ F を選び、○をつけましょう。

	答え
① The writer argues that many people in Japan do not want to change the situation surrounding LGBT people because there is no oppression against homosexuals at all in Japan.	T ・ F
② In both Japan and the United States, homosexuality is portrayed in novels and films.	T ・ F
③ According to the writer, American men are more likely to prefer stories that depict male-male romance to those that depict male-female romance.	T ・ F
④ The writer says that men are more likely to discriminate against homosexuals than women because they want to deny the homosexual tendencies within themselves.	T ・ F
⑤ "Bromance" refers to a relationship between men who are as close as brothers, including sexual relations.	T ・ F
⑥ There are no innovative gay films in Japanese cinema, and characters often follow the old gay image.	T ・ F
⑦ In Japan, gay entertainers tend to provoke laughter by making themselves the object of ridicule.	T ・ F

EXERCISE ④：Word Order --

文構造と文の意味を意識しながら、次の［　　］内の表現を並べ替えて、文法的にも意味的にも正しい文を作りましょう。

① "Hate crimes" [as / acts / slander / defined as / such / are / illegal], threats, and assaults based on prejudice or negative feelings about a particular race, color, religion, ethnicity, nationality, gender, age, or disability.

② In 1998, Matthew Shepard, a college student in Wyoming, [men / being gay / by / for / two / severely assaulted / was] and died five days later.

③ "Bromance" is a portmanteau of brother and romance, [men / between / emotionally connected / close relationship / a / two / indicating].

④ "We [should / that same-sex / had / recognize / have / do / couples / the rights] long ago," said the Parliamentary Undersecretary of the country, which legalized same-sex marriage and adoption by same-sex couples in January 2023.

⑤ The Tokyo District Court ruled that [the Constitution / does not / of same-sex / of recognition / violate / current lack / marriage in Japan], but noted that the absence of a legal system for same-sex partners to become family members is an unconstitutional state of affairs.

⑥ As of 2023, Japan [recognize / that / among / the only / is / same-sex marriage / does not / country] the G-7 countries, but the situation regarding same-sex marriage may change in the U.S. in the near future, as U.S. courts are also swinging to the conservative side.

⑦ Some countries still [impose / stoning / criminal / that / by / laws in force / the death penalty / have] for homosexual acts; in short, people throw stones at "criminals" until they die from the injuries.

EXERCISE ⑤ : Discussion／Writing

次の問いかけに関して、自分の考えをまとめてみましょう。

① Some oppose same-sex marriage on the grounds that it will destabilize traditional society, while others are in favor of same-sex marriage on the grounds that allowing same-sex marriage will not change society at all, but will only make gay people happier. What is your opinion on this issue and explain why.

② What do you think about same-sex married couples adopting children? Please explain your thoughts along with your reasons.

Chapter 15 The Age of Diversity

精神的な自由は、人間が生まれつき持つ権利ですが、これは単に心の中の自由が認められているということではありません。自分の信念や思想に基づいて発言したり行動したりする自由がなければ、心の自由に意味はありません。多様な生き方が認められる社会になりつつあるように見えますが、まだまだ、言論や行動の自由が侵害される事例が起こっています。そのような問題と関連させながら、本章の内容を考えましょう。

PRE-EXERCISE

次の英語の映画タイトルから内容を推測しながら、語群の日本語タイトルと結びつけ、答えを書き入れましょう。

	答え		答え
① *The Post*（2017）		④ *Frozen*（2013）	
② *The Conductor*（2018）		⑤ *12 Years a Slave*（2013）	
③ *Bicentennial Man*（1999）		⑥ *On the Basis of Sex*（2018）	

語群

a.『アンドリューNDR114』　　b.『ペンタゴン・ペーパーズ—最高機密文書—』
c.『ビリーブ　未来への大逆転』　　d.『レディ・マエストロ』
e.『アナと雪の女王』　　f.『それでも夜は明ける』

EXERCISE ①

次の文章はリーディング箇所で扱われている映画のあらすじです。文構造や文意を考えながら音声を聴いて、下線部に表現を書き入れてみましょう。

映画❶：『流浪の月』（*Wandering*）

One evening in a rainy park, Fumi, a 19-year-old college student, meets a 10-year-old girl（1）＿＿＿＿＿＿ Sarasa. Sarasa, who lives with her aunt, does not want to go home, so Fumi takes her home. They（2）＿＿＿＿＿＿ two months in Fumi's room, and eventually Fumi is（3）＿＿＿＿＿＿ for kidnapping Sarasa. Fumi and Sarasa, now "the kidnapper" and "the girl victim" in the eyes of the public, meet again 15 years after the（4）＿＿＿＿＿＿.

映画❷：『コーダ』（*CODA*）

> Ruby, a high school student, lives with her parents and brother, who have hearing (1)_____. Ruby has been helping them as a sign-language (2)_____. She is a talented singer, which her choir club advisor notices. He (3)_____ her to apply to a prestigious music college. However, her parents cannot understand and oppose the idea, since they cannot hear her sing. After much (4)_____, Ruby decides to give up on her dream.

ⒺXERCISE ②

次の英語表現と最も意味の近い日本語表現を語群から選び、答えを書き入れてみましょう。

	答え		答え		答え
① milestone		⑥ feature		⑪ confine	
② stand for		⑦ depiction		⑫ victim	
③ additionally		⑧ on the contrary		⑬ suffer from	
④ openly		⑨ dual		⑭ coexist	
⑤ attitude		⑩ emphasize		⑮ diversity	

語群

a. 被害者　　　　　b. それに加えて　　　c. 共存する
d. 態度　　　　　　e. 多様性　　　　　　f. 限る、制限する
g. …を象徴する　　h. 節目となるもの　　i. 二重の
j. それとは反対に　k. （病気）で苦しむ　l. 強調する
m. 描写　　　　　　n. …を主演させる　　o. 公に

ⓇEADING

The 2022 Academy Awards ceremony was a **milestone** showing Hollywood's willingness to honor those previously discriminated against.

First, the Best Picture award went to *Coda*. Its title, *Coda*, **stands for** Children of Deaf Adults. The Best Director award was presented to Jane Campion for *The Power of the Dog*, only the third female director to win the award. The Best Leading actor award went to Will Smith for his role in *King Richard*, making him the fifth black actor to win the prize. The Best Supporting Actor award went to Troy Kotsur for his role as the father in *Coda*, the first deaf man to win the award. Marlee Matlin, who also appears in *Coda*, was the first deaf woman to win the Best Supporting Actress award for *Children of a Lesser God* in 1986. **Additionally**, Ariana DeBose of *West Side Story* is the first **openly** LGBT person to win the Best Supporting Actress award. It was truly an awards ceremony that demonstrated Hollywood's **attitude** of not discriminating against minorities.

It has been less than 20 years since *Brokeback Mountain*, which **features** gay men, caused a fuss about "gay discrimination" at the Oscars, as it missed out on Best Picture while winning Best Director. In the past, so-called gay films were stereotypical in their **depiction** of gay people. Gay men were portrayed as feminine, holding up their pinkies when holding a glass, cross-dressing, speaking in a ladylike manner, etc. Or, **on the contrary**, they were portrayed as macho, boasting of their beautiful muscles and being conscious of being stared at. In terms of profession, they were usually fashion designers and hairdressers. However, as you might expect, such conventional depictions have become increasingly boring to audiences. Gay films are steadily evolving.

*fuss：喧噪、騒ぎ

Brokeback Mountain was groundbreaking in its portrayal of some real-life gay men instead of stereotypes. The film can be considered a "gayification" of the traditional Western movies of the past. After watching this film, every time I watch Western movies from around the 1950s, the heyday of the Western, I cannot help but wonder whether the heroes of the past were also secretly gay. It seems these films made people feel and aware of the existence of sexuality that had not yet been named. This film, on the other hand, was a story of an "impermissible love" which cannot be outwardly expressed due to homophobic fears.

Eleven years later, in 2016, *Moonlight* won Best Picture despite addressing the **dual** discrimination of being gay and black. In this film, again, the characters are not stereotyped. The protagonist is set up as a bullied child, a feminine lad, who becomes a muscle-bound, macho drug trafficker when he grows up. The transition from feminine boy to macho, muscle man might be described as a gay male stereotype, but this aspect of the film is not underscored. Rather, the film is more memorable for the line from his mentor, Juan played by Mahershala Ali, who assures him, "You can be gay, but... you don't have to let nobody call you a faggot." The film is less about the struggles of being born gay but rather the life story of an individual man, who happens to be gay and

*nobody：文法的には anybody。
*faggot：同性愛者に対する差別的・侮蔑的表現。

black. Being gay is only one element that makes up the character.

Green Book, another Best Picture winner, is a road movie about a gay black artist and his Italian chauffeur, in which sexuality is never **emphasized**. Rather, it is a film that impresses us with the ridiculousness of the social system. Here, too, being gay is shown as just one of the elements making up a human being.

*chauffeur：お抱え運転手

The Power of the Dog, just like *Brokeback Mountain*, can be considered a "gayification" of the evergreen Western hero, but the word "gay" is not even in it. The film features a savage man and traces his life with exceptional direction, but many audiences may have finished watching the film without realizing his gayness. Being gay is just one of the factors that constitute an individual person.

If you trace the history of cinema, you will find that, until the removal of the Hays Code in 1968, the blatant depiction of gays was a taboo in the film industry, but even before that time, Hollywood films had hinted at the existence of sexual minorities, using a coded approach. The documentary film *The Celluloid Closet* unravels how homosexuality was secretly portrayed as seeming heterosexuality in the days before the ban was lifted.

It is worth noting that some people's view of gay people as unique and special has been fading away over the course of time. People have also come to recognize that human sexuality is actually diverse.

Japanese cinema is also steadily undergoing an evolution. *Wandering* (*The Wandering Moon*) is a good example of a film that is not **confined** to traditional ideas and depictions. In the film, a man, played by Tori Matsuzaka, kidnaps a baby girl. However, it does not simply portray the abduction of a girl as just a crime. The kidnapping **victim**, played by Suzu Hirose, feels more at ease when she is with him.

In fact, she is also a victim of domestic violence. In domestic violence, generally, people with low self-esteem seem to be more likely to be targeted and victimized. She has low self-esteem and so does he. Thus, those with low self-esteem are attracted to each other. In the end, the kidnapper's illness is revealed, and the scene is extremely meaningful.

He **suffers from** a disease called Klinefelter's Syndrome. Only about one in 660 people have this disease. Yet many people, even those studying LGBTQIA+, may not be familiar with it. The film, too, does not explain the details of the disease, but only hints that it is a serious illness. However, the audience will be able to understand the anguish and sadness of belonging to a minority, even if it is only implied.

*anguish：はなはだ しい苦しみ、苦悶

The era in which we live is precisely the era of minorities. We are expected to understand and **coexist** with minorities rather than excluding them from our society. All human beings are different in some way. Is there such a thing as a "normal" person in the world? Differences are individuality. Coexistence with **diversity** is definitely a key phrase for the future.

EXERCISE ③ --
次の各文が、リーディングの内容と一致していれば T を、一致しなければ F を選び、〇をつけましょう。

	答え
① The directors and actors honored at the 2022 Academy Awards represented a range of minorities.	T・F
② The Academy Awards have traditionally honored films depicting minority people.	T・F
③ Films dealing with gay life and winning Academy Awards have often been the subject of criticism.	T・F
④ In films such as *Moonlight* and *Green Book*, sexual identity is represented as a part of human character.	T・F
⑤ The way minorities were portrayed in some films was stereotypical, but that is changing.	T・F
⑥ Japanese and American films differ in many ways in their attitudes toward minorities.	T・F
⑦ We need to separate those who are a minority because they have a disease from those who are a minority because of their sexual preference.	T・F

EXERCISE ④ : Word Order

文構造と文の意味を意識しながら、次の〔　　〕内の表現を並べ替えて、文法的にも意味的にも正しい文を作りましょう。文頭に来る文字も選択肢では小文字になっています。

① 〔 mean / does not / minority / majority vote / deciding by / that 〕 opinions can be ignored.

② Women are not a minority, but 〔 for a / subject to / been / they / discrimination / have 〕 long time.

③ Some of 〔 shortly after the / who /the new coronavirus infection / outbreak of / were / became infected / those 〕 severely discriminated against.

④ One of the advantages 〔 us / it / experience / of watching / to / movies / is that / allows 〕 diverse lives.

⑤ While our direct experience is limited, 〔 expand / about / learning / the / our knowledge / can / infinitely by / we 〕 experiences of others.

⑥ 〔 the characters in / may / we / empathize with / reveal / are able to / the work / whether or not 〕 a prejudice that we are unaware of.

⑦ Tragically, 〔 revealed / are / until / is / some cases of / not / the worst / child abuse 〕 over.

EXERCISE ⑤：Discussion／Writing

次の問いかけに関して、自分の考えをまとめてみましょう。

① Respect for diversity has been emphasized in the media in recent years, yet discriminatory expressions and ideas that are difficult to notice have entered various media. Examine movies, TV dramas, advertisements, etc., and point out examples that are discriminatory along with examples that promote respect for diversity.

② Examine the meaning and history of the concepts of "democracy" and "human rights" and consider how these relate to respect for diversity.

［日本語エッセイ執筆］伊藤公雄、國友万裕

［監修・執筆］安田優、松本恵美、轟里香
［執筆］Lisa Miller、朴育美、長岡亜生、仲川浩世、船本弘史、後藤リサ
　　　　須田久美子、奥村玲香、チアノ典子、友田奈津子、杉原由里子
　　　　豊島知穂、今井朋子

テキストの音声は、弊社 HP　https://www.eihosha.co.jp/
の「テキスト音声ダウンロード」のバナーからダウンロードできます。
また、下記 QR コードを読み込み、音声ファイルをダウンロードするか、
ストリーミングページにジャンプして音声を聴くことができます。

Let's look into various issues in Japan
and America through films !
映画で見るジェンダー

2024 年 1 月 15 日　初 版

編 著 者 © 安 　 田 　 　 優

発 行 者 　佐 々 木 　 元

発 行 所 　株式会社 　英 　 宝 　 社
〒 101-0032 東京都千代田区岩本町 2-7-7
電話 03-5833-5870　FAX03-5833-5872
https://www.eihosha.co.jp/

ISBN 978-4-269-11043-4 C1082
印刷：日本ハイコム株式会社／製本：有限会社井上製本所